The 8 Traits of Champion Golfers

○
△

Dr. Deborah Graham
and Jon Stabler

Simon & Schuster

SIMON & SCHUSTER
Rockefeller Center
1230 Avenue of the Americas
New York, NY 10020

Designed by Meryl Sussman Levavi/digitext, inc.
Manufactured in the United States of America

1   3   5   7   9   10   8   6   4   2

Library of Congress Cataloging-in-Publication Data
is available

ISBN 0-684-85631-X

Acknowledgments

Because we are influenced by the greatness of those around us, it is impossible to acknowledge all who help choreograph our direction and lend to our accomplishments. When challenged to choose but a few, I first want to thank my mother, for instilling in me a commitment to who and what I love—including a love for sport. Then I must thank my daddy, Jack Graham, and coaches, Charles McFarland and Gerry Shudde, for showing me how fishing and sport can so completely enrich a life. And Dr. Richard Lister, for introducing me to a wonderful career in psychology and, even better, a way to combine it with my love of sport—he enlightens me endlessly with his wisdom, enthusiasm, and sporting adventures. Also my husband, Jon—my best friend, tennis partner, and most honorable person I know—for believing in me, loving me unconditionally, and being a great partner in every possible way . . . including writing this book.

Beyond these and the countless other important people who have influenced my life and career, there are the many great people in the world of golf who have made our work in the sport possible. Many thanks to all the touring professionals, their spouses and families, who have so graciously invited us into their lives and who, in many cases, have also become great friends. Also the PGA, Senior PGA, LPGA, and Nike Tour officials, and the Centinella Hospital Tour fitness staff for embracing our efforts and for making our work easier. Also the many amateurs, college coaches and teams, junior golfers, club professionals and teachers, who have allowed us to share with them our collective wisdom about the mental game of golf.

At least, a word of thanks must also go to all the people at Simon & Schuster involved with this book, especially Jeff Neuman for his support even during his time of deep personal loss; and to our own office manager, Susan Hartin, for all her helpful research. Finally to my nephew, Archie, for understanding my need to dominate the home computer; to my friends Grace Yasmineh and Jacque Chaney, for always caring how "it" was going; and last but not least, my devoted dog, Kiki, for lying right by my side through the entire project. Now we are both going to get back in shape.

This book is dedicated to the life and memory of my mother, Della Jane (Reitzer) Holland. The love, support, and dedication she imparted as a mother, grandmother, aunt, wife, and friend supercedes her short life.

Contents

The 8 Traits of Champion Golfers

Introduction:
The GolfPsych Way

"In 1993, my second year on the Senior PGA Tour, I won five tournaments and $1,175,944, was leading money-winner, and was named Player of the Year. Yes, I made some physical improvements in my game, but the main reason I had a year that for me was unbelievable is that I worked hard on the mental side of my game. Two years earlier I had begun working with Dr. Deborah Graham . . . and with her help . . . worked very hard to improve the mental deficiencies that were keeping me from playing my best."

Dave Stockton, June 1994

It was a warm summer day in Carmel, Indiana. Tension and excitement filled the air. The 1991 PGA Championship was about to be played at Pete Dye's Crooked Stick Golf Course, and even though it was only Tuesday, two days before play would begin for real, you could feel the anticipation among the players.

Dave Stockton was one of those players. At the age of

forty-nine, he was taking advantage of the lifetime exemption he'd earned by winning the PGA in 1970. For good measure, he won it again in 1976, but this upcoming PGA meant more for Dave than it did years ago, or than it did for many of the "youngsters" in the field who were nearly half his age. Less than three months later, on November 1, 1991, he would turn fifty and join the Senior PGA Tour. This tournament represented the end of one and the beginning of another competitive golf career.

Dave had been one of the top players on the PGA Tour from 1967 to 1978 as the winner of eleven events. But in the 1980s, rather than continue to wrestle with the strain and guilt of constantly leaving his wife, Cathy, and his sons, David and Ronnie, at home to play in events lasting five or six days, he adopted a "corporate" career, teaching golf to America's business leaders at about ninety brief outings a year. By 1991, however, the children were adults—his son Dave, Jr., now plays on the PGA Tour—and Cathy could come out on Tour whenever she wanted. So he'd started to cut back on his corporate schedule to concentrate more on actually playing the game. In between preparing for the 1991 Ryder Cup—he was to captain the U.S. squad in the matches that fall—he'd been working long and hard on his game. After all, a new beginning beckoned.

I first met Dave when he was being treated for a nagging wrist injury in the Centinela Fitness Trailer, a large rig filled with exercise equipment and staffed by certified trainers that follows the Senior Tour. We were introduced by Paul Azinger, one of Dave's Ryder Cup team members. I and my husband, Jon, had known Paul for several years as he had been one of the first male players to fill out a "GolfPsych" personality profile for us. This profile allowed us to determine strengths and weaknesses in Paul's game, and the introduction came about because Paul suggested to Dave that he might make a more fruitful return to competition if he, too, would fill out a profile and go over the results with us. Within a minute of our meeting, Dave said he was interested in learning more about himself.

The GolfPsych profile is based on the "Cattell 16 Personality Factor" questionnaire developed and revised over the years by Dr. Raymond Cattell, one of this country's leading researchers in personality and psychology. The Cattell 16 PF test is today widely used in psychology to measure personalities. It asks 187 questions and gives measures of thirty-two different personality traits on sixteen bipolar scales—which is to say, each scale measures two traits that are the opposite of each other, so that a single measurement is valid. For example, "relaxed" is the opposite of "tense," so measuring how relaxed someone is also tells you how tense that person is.

In 1981, for my doctoral thesis, I decided to determine if there were differences between the personalities of what we called "champion" women professional golfers and other women professional golfers (not to mention other women in general). The Cattell 16 PF test already had been used successfully to identify common and differing traits among many other groups. For example, one investigation compared non-athlete cadets with athletes in the U.S. Air Force Academy and found the latter to be more rule-bound, tough-minded, analytic, self-sufficient, and self-controlled. I suspected a similar study could be done with women's golf.

I also felt that if one could identify the traits of champion women golfers, then theoretically those who were *not* champions would know which areas of their personalities needed "work" in order for them to become champions. Many people had known for a long time that a sound mental game was important to playing well. I was interested in the specifics of this process.

With the help of LPGA Hall-of-Famer Carol Mann and Jim Hardy, at that time a teacher who worked with many LPGA players, I got access to more than fifty LPGA touring professionals. They took the test. The results were then grouped based on career records and performances in major championships. The champion group was composed of frequent winners. The near-champion group had won once or twice and had been on Tour for many years. The nonchampion group had been on Tour for many years but had never won.

After the test scores had been broken down using several accepted computer-analysis programs, it became clear that eight of the thirty-two personality trait scores were distinctly different for the champion group versus the other two groups. Here are the eight traits as defined by Dr. Cattell's bipolar scales. (Note: We've underlined the champion traits and have provided the official names used by GolfPsych.)

1. <u>Reserved or Cool</u> vs. Outgoing or Warm: We define this trait as "Focus."
2. Concrete Thinking vs. <u>Abstract Thinking:</u> We define it as "Abstract Thinking."
3. Affected by Feelings vs. <u>Emotional Stability:</u> We define it as "Emotional Stability."
4. Submissive vs. <u>Dominant:</u> We define it as "Dominance."
5. Tender-minded vs. <u>Tough-minded:</u> We define it as "Tough-mindedness."
6. Apprehensive vs. <u>Confident:</u> We define it as "Confidence."
7. Group-oriented vs. <u>Self-sufficient:</u> We define it as "Self-sufficiency."
8. Relaxed vs. Tense: We define it as "Optimum Arousal." Notice there is no underline; that's because the champion trait is a nice balance between the two ends of the scale.

In 1988 and 1989 we took the study to the PGA Tour and the Senior PGA Tour. When we analyzed those results, the same champion traits appeared, albeit with slightly different measures, or "scores." This is not to say that male champion golfers and female champion golfers have the same exact personalities because, as you shall see, a personality is a mix of all the individual traits, and no two mixes are exactly alike. But all the champions scored reasonably consistently across these eight traits.

We had finally hit upon "The Eight Traits of Champion Golfers."

It is important to remember when reading this book that we usually describe the "statistical" or "perfect" champion in our profile discussions. But in golf, as in life, no one is perfect, with the ideal measures of each trait on each bipolar scale. Such players as Dave Stockton, Lee Janzen, and many great amateur and club players definitely come close. But that's only after identifying and working on their weaknesses.

We have a broad client base of players of all abilities and from all walks of golfing life, including touring professionals, club professionals, public and private club players, amateurs, college players, and juniors. At *each* level we see players improve their games by strengthening their weaker personality traits. Perhaps more important, not only do they improve their scores, but they also *enjoy* the game more. Many even report that the changes they made for golf improved their personal lives as well—which, of course, is *our* main goal. People's lives are enhanced when confidence improves, their stress is managed, and they become more decisive, better organized, and simply more aware.

We give each client the complete Cattell 16 PF test, then compile a 50-page "GolfPsych Report" that describes the eight champion trait scores and their relevance to golf. It discusses the scores and how they compare to the champion golfers. It also tells what implications those scores have. We then summarize their scores on a one-page GolfPsych Profile and make personalized recommendations for the player.

This book does not contain the complete test, but we have included some simple evaluation techniques to get you started on the way to improving your life and your golf game. We also give you examples of actual recommendations that have been submitted to various clients and the evidence of our program's success. Several case studies of golfers of different abilities allow easy comparison of your profile and that of a champion golfer. One such case is Dave Stockton, who, as we mentioned before, wanted to learn more about himself as he prepared to join the Senior Tour.

I gave Dave the test packet and asked that he return it to me the next day so we could review the results that week. As his starting times were late Thursday and early Friday, we made an appointment for Friday afternoon.

Dave played so well the first day—shooting a 71 and putting him in good position to make the thirty-six-hole cut— that I wondered if he would keep the appointment. Because they are very self-sufficient, professional golfers often decide to talk to sport psychologists about their games only when they are frustrated with their play; then, they decide to cancel after a good round, figuring they've sorted things out. Once they realize the bad habits or frustrations are still there, they set up another appointment. Knowing Dave as well as I know him now, I should have expected no less than a full commitment to his decision. When I saw him in the Crooked Stick clubhouse on Thursday evening, he returned his responses to the questionnaire. He couldn't help but show his excitement about the day's success, yet he cheerfully suggested we meet the following day near the first tee box after the last afternoon group played through.

Dave's second round did not go so well; he shot a 77. By the time we met, it was all but certain that he'd missed the cut. This probably made Dave even more open-minded to our initial discussion, and it gave us fresh examples of how his personality and habits of thought were both positively and negatively affecting his play.

In many ways, golf is like a microcosm of life in that it can magnify your personality. In a single round you can experience a full range of emotions, personal challenges, and tests of character—far more than you might experience in a routine week at work or at home. It's why many business executives have made a round of golf an important medium for getting to know someone before offering or making a deal.

When we sat down to talk, I explained to Dave that our first aim was to review his personality profile and compare his scores to the GolfPsych Profile. Then, using the eight traits of champion golfers, we'd set specific goals for strengthening his mental game.

Because the profile reflects a person's general personality, I told him it would help to discuss specific problems he experienced during competition. This would help us determine if he changed his personality when playing golf, either intentionally or unintentionally and for the better or worse for his game.

Before beginning, I also emphasized to Dave that three important factors could enhance the value of our discussion and its relevance to him.

1. *There are no "perfect" champions.* After testing all levels of players on the PGA, Senior PGA, and LPGA Tours, we found that everyone has some area of his or her personality that can be strengthened for golf. While the champions come closer to scoring within close range of all eight traits, we found that all players have Achilles heels, weaker areas that can detract from their strengths. For one player this may be extreme self-consciousness—he worries too much—while another may sometimes lose concentration. Others may be too excitable or too aggressive. Usually at least one of these traits needs to be controlled if a golfer wants to perform at his peak.

2. *The eight traits of champion golfers affect one another.* They are part of a "formula," and the fluctuation of one trait can affect the strength or weakness of the others. For example, someone may be good at focusing over the ball. If, for whatever reason, that golfer gets too emotional or tense, he likely will not be able

to focus properly. And if that person works on focusing without working on relaxation or managing his emotions, he may never play at his peak. To get the most out of your efforts, it is important to identify the real cause of the mental weakness and to strengthen that weakness so the other traits can blossom.

3. *Physical effort seldom solves mental problems.* When a golfer misses a tee shot because too much tension affected his posture, rhythm, swing plane, or other fundamentals, he's more likely to try to make a physical correction than use his mental skills to lower his tension. Instead of solving the *real* problem, he spends the entire round working on his swing and getting more tense, instead of relaxing and giving his trained and natural swing a real chance to execute. By the end of the round, he'll be exhausted, confused, and worst of all, feel little or no confidence in what were probably sound fundamentals to begin with.

Dave especially appreciated the third fact. He revealed that he'd long felt his physical game, particularly off the tee, was not as good as many of his rivals on the Tour and that his success was largely a result of his efforts to think well on the course. "That's why I'm here at Crooked Stick," he said. "I know my time to practice and play are limited. I'll be really involved with the Ryder Cup through September, which will leave me only a month to work on my game before my first Senior event in November. And I want to be mentally ready so I can get the most out of my game when I do become eligible for the Senior Tour. Besides, he added, "whatever I learn here just may help us bring home the Cup." True to his competitive personality, Dave was looking for an edge in the Ryder Cup as well.

I knew little about Dave except that he was to be the Ryder Cup captain, he was one of the best players in the 1970s, and based on his profile, an intelligent, hard working, organized, conscientious, and competitive professional. I had a hunch that this was going to be an interesting and fun session.

In the three hours that followed, Dave proved my hunch correct. We assessed how his personality could both help and hinder his competitiveness. We took one trait at a time, discussed its relevance to golf, and explored how Dave could use it best. Once we had covered every trait, we set a number of goals that would allow Dave to play the best golf of his life. What follows is a summary of our conversation, trait by trait, and the resulting goals for each of the eight traits. (The individual chapters of this book will take you through each trait in detail, and as a result, you'll be able to pinpoint the strongest and weakest parts of your game.)

FOCUS

After discussing his previous round and his specific thoughts immediately prior to missing shots, it became evident that Dave's focus over the ball was irregular: sometimes great, sometimes skewed. His test scores indicated he had a natural ability to narrow his focus to concentrate, but it appeared that the years of corporate outings, which involved entertaining, conversing, and teaching—activities that, if anything, discourage focus—had left him with mental habits unsuited for competitive golf. He sometimes hit shots while thinking of a conversation he'd just had or while still mentally involved with whatever was going on around him at the time.

This is much the same problem that teaching professionals experience with their own games when they go from the lesson tee or their pro shops into a competitive environment. Business professionals face a similar problem as they rush from the office to the first tee. It's difficult to detach from the details and distractions of the business world and focus.

Fortunately the skewed focus was only moderately evident during Dave's first round, largely because he came into the event rested, happy, and expecting little of his game except to start conditioning himself for competition. His thoughts changed during his second round, however. The previous day's play had charged him with hope, anticipation, and expectation, all of which further widened his focus. In hindsight, Dave realized that he thought much more about score and position while hitting shots during his second round, and that seemed to open the door to thinking too much about his competitors, their scores, the cut, who was watching, how he compared to other players, and so on.

I explained to Dave that one of the eight traits demonstrated by champion golfers is an above-average ability to narrow their focus over the ball and detach from everything going on around them, no matter what the circumstance. I further explained that narrowing this focus also meant detaching from internal distractions, high expectations, and over-involvement with results.

Champions also are good at relaxing this focus *between* shots, then narrowing it again as they approach the ball, thinking about only the shot or putt at hand. This clarity of thought can come more easily to the player who has inner peace and who has some introverted tendencies, but all players can learn to improve their concentration over the ball if they identify their own deterrents and learn the simple mental skills proven effective for enhancing focus.

Growing up as an only child, Dave had some introverted tendencies; you can see traces of them today in the way he's perfectly comfortable being alone when he's practicing or hunting or fishing. But he learned to be more extroverted during his corporate career and his tournament play as he became comfortable meeting, entertaining, and teaching large groups of people or mixing with other pro golfers. I wanted Dave to understand that he had an edge on players who are true extroverts and that, with a little practice, he could be one of the best both at maintaining focus under even the most difficult circumstances and at relaxing that focus between shots. As successful golf ultimately involves hitting a golf ball, we would work first on his ability to narrow his focus.

I told Dave that the most important step a player can take

toward strengthening his abilities to focus is to learn and discipline himself to use a strong mental routine. His response was similar to that of many of my golfing clients, both professional and amateur: "I have a good physical routine, but I'm not sure I have a good mental routine. In fact, I'm really not sure what a good mental routine is." I told Dave that he probably has some kind of mental routine, though he probably doesn't call on it when he most needs it, either because he is not as aware of his thoughts as he could be when he approaches the ball or he has not defined his best thoughts for executing each shot.

The aim was for Dave to treat every shot the same and give each total concentration. Most players find that maintaining this kind of focus is most difficult on those days of extremes, when their physical play is either really good or really bad. On the good days, concentration can fall victim to excitement, anticipation, expectation, or even the fear of success. On bad days, it can be lost to frustration, anger, mechanical thoughts, or fear of embarrassment by poor play. I therefore gave Dave a three-step mental routine and asked him to incorporate it into his game. It's a routine that has helped each of our clients narrow their focus and maximize use of their natural and trained athletic abilities and skills.

ABSTRACT THINKING

Abstract thinking is a simple measure of intelligence as defined by Dr. Cattell. We refer to it as the golfer's ability to analytically reason, problem-solve, learn, and adapt intellectually.

Dave's profile showed him to be of above-average intelligence, which can be both good and bad news to a competitive golfer. On the positive side, abstract thinking skills can give a tremendous edge when it comes time to develop strategies for playing difficult courses under difficult conditions. Adding and subtracting yardages is easy, as is adjusting to changing conditions or reading difficult greens. But high abstract thinking will make it easier to learn new skills and to gain a greater understanding of one's own game. When Dave, a good abstract thinker, is "off" mechanically, he can generally diagnose the problem quickly and find a solution.

On the negative side, an abstract thinker's intellect can quickly get him into trouble because he'll often overthink a situation. This could involve seeing breaks that don't exist in a green, overanalyzing a missed shot, or spending unnecessary time calculating scores and positions.

Golf, I explained to Dave, is one of the most difficult sports to master not because it involves hitting a small ball long distances and having to do so accurately, but more because of the extreme *mental* disciplines required. One such mental discipline involves playing with a quiet, peaceful mind. This is extremely difficult to do in golf because of the large amounts of idle time between shots. That downtime allows ample opportunity to get down on yourself, analyze and fret over your mistakes, fear failure, and otherwise sabotage yourself mentally. So much for a quiet and peaceful mind.

Another mental discipline involves overcoming the simple fact that it's easier to use our natural and trained abilities only when we can *intuitively* hit a ball rather than when we analytically study how to hit it. That's why it's easier to hit a softball with a bat even though the ball is moving when you hit it. In golf, the ball sits squarely in front of you and you start to analyze and think. When you hit a softball, you are reacting to the ball rather than analyzing how to do so.

The more intelligent you are, the more important it is to clear your mind between shots and simplify your thoughts over the ball. This was Dave's problem during his second round. He wasted too much thought on calculating the cut, analyzing missed shots, and assessing how he would finish based on how he anticipated playing the holes ahead. He'd have fared much better had he focused only on hitting the shot.

So that gave Dave a few more challenges: Learn skills for

quieting the mind, learn to play more with feel than analysis, and learn to keep his thoughts "in the moment."

EMOTIONAL STABILITY

Dave scored well here, falling in the same range of emotional stability as the best players, which is to say he showed a slightly above-average ability to stay emotionally stable despite life's ups and downs. We discussed whether he tended to remain stable when he competed or if he experienced mood swings involving fear, anger, frustration, disappointment, excitement, elation, and anticipation.

Dave appeared to be very good at managing his emotions, except when he started making *results* too important—as most golfers are prone to do. His second round was a good example of his putting too much emphasis on results. He wasn't concerned with hitting good shots because good shots naturally lead to good results. He was concerned with hitting good shots because he wanted to make the cut. In his first round he had just emphasized using the smoothest swing possible on each shot, finding the ball, and doing it again.

Emotional swings were not as big a problem for Dave as they are for many players. We did, however, agree on a difficult and challenging goal of trying to emphasize simply hitting shots and stroking putts rather than focusing on the actual outcomes of these shots.

DOMINANCE

The fourth of the eight traits of champion golfers measures how submissive and easygoing a golfer is versus how aggressive, dominant, and competitive he is. Dave scored *exactly* where the champions measured, which is to say he was slightly above average in the dominance trait. This gives Dave an advantage in that he is most likely to manage the course with a strategy that maximizes his skills. He is also enough of a risk taker to give himself an opportunity to score, yet he is not so aggressive that he tries to force opportunities with low-percentage shots.

Players who are too submissive tend to manage the course too conservatively or play defensively, seldom getting the most out of their skills. This often results in high scores coming immediately after low scores and a tendency to play poorly when in the lead. Players who are too dominant, on the other hand, have a compulsion to overpower the course—or their shots—and often get themselves into trouble.

The goal we set for Dave was for him to develop a moderately aggressive game plan before each round—especially before the first. When he pointed out that he already did this, I asked him to refuse to change the plan based on his score—especially when that would mean playing more aggressively to make up strokes. "This," he said, "I can improve. When I try to make up strokes or force an opportunity, it usually costs me."

TOUGH-MINDEDNESS

It became apparent during my visit with Dave that he was a tender-minded and caring individual. He spoke endearingly of his wife and sons for whom he had quit the PGA Tour so he could spend more time with them. This also was reflected in the ways he described relating to other people, including his fellow professionals.

A tender-minded person is sensitive to other people and their needs, showing courtesy, thoughtfulness, and compassion. The tough-minded individual is at the other extreme. This person remains self-centered, indifferent, and unmoved by the needs of those around him.

We found that champion golfers test above average in their abilities to remain tough-minded. This means they're not distracted by sensitivities to the thoughts and feelings of others when they compete. A tough-minded player doesn't care what other players might think of his swing or how unhappy friends and/or playing partners might be with their own poor play.

There are advantages and disadvantages to being very tough-minded. The advantage is in competition, where little focus is lost to concerns for others or to worries about bad weather and other conditions. The disadvantage is in interpersonal relationships, where a lack of compassion can inhibit or greatly strain or even destroy personal bonds.

My personal view of a champion is someone who can be tough-minded on the golf course yet tender-minded in relationships that are important to him. Dave is that person, although he tested to be a bit more tender-minded than the statistical champion. It became evident that he could benefit from being more tough-minded in competition.

Granted, he was a bit out of practice at being tough-minded, since he hadn't competed in a while. Plus, Dave is the sort of person who truly enjoys helping other players with their games and will sometimes forgo his own practice to do so. We discussed reversing this priority when he was preparing for competition so that he was sure to take care of his own needs first.

There also were times when Dave would find himself less focused on his own game because he was concerned about the struggles of a playing partner. Dave agreed he could better conserve his attention and mental energies for himself by not getting as emotionally involved with the games of his playing partners. He would instead make mental notes of suggestions or support he might want to offer *after* the round—and then put them aside until he was finished.

By now Dave was pretty excited. He said he was starting to understand how his personality influenced his thoughts and how his thoughts influenced his play. Just knowing where to start working on his mental game made him eager to compete. But I reminded him that there were a few more traits to review before his goal setting would be complete, and that each of the traits had to work with the others in the "formula" we'd talked of at the beginning of our consultation, the formula that requires *all* the mental aspects be seen as interconnected.

CONFIDENCE

As we proceeded with Dave's profile, his score revealed that confidence was definitely not one of his weaknesses. Like other champions, he tested well above average on self-assurance, indicating that he had a healthy, secure, self-satisfied view of himself.

Confidence is vital in golf because the game can quickly and easily crush an apprehensive player. Unfortunately, confidence can be one of the most difficult traits to strengthen because it takes both time and a strong commitment to change.

At this point, Dave told me that he had spent considerable time before his first PGA Championship victory, 1970, at Southern Hills Country Club in Tulsa, trying to raise his confidence through the use of positive thinking and positive imagery. He happened upon a book called *Psycho-Cybernetics* by Dr. Maxwell Maltz—one of the early self-help books that has remained popular since its original publication in the 1960s.

Dave explained that the book motivated him to spend considerable time visualizing himself playing in contention, with complete confidence in his abilities to play well under pressure. It worked. At the beginning of the last day of that PGA Championship, Dave got into contention by playing consistent golf.

There was a near disaster on the thirteenth hole, however, when Dave dumped his second shot into a pond short of the green. But he called on his positive imagery, quickly regrouped, and hit a wedge to within inches to save bogey. His confidence then allowed him to hold off both Arnold Palmer and Bob Murphy. He actually imagined himself walking confidently onto the eighteenth green leading the tournament, with a vague acknowledgment of the cheering crowd surrounding him. As he found himself in that exact situation on the final hole, he had the comfortable feeling of having been there before. He won by two strokes.

So I did not have to convince Dave of the importance of strong confidence or of the power of positive imagery. I did want to explain to him, however, that to get the most out of his confidence, it would be important to recognize that there are two types of confidence, and both must be maintained in competition. There is "personal confidence," which is a healthy respect for, and belief in, yourself, and there is "performance confidence," which reflects your current belief in your golf skills.

Even though his personal confidence tested strongly, we needed to discuss performance confidence. I needed to know if Dave lacked confidence in any part of his game at that moment. "Yes, my driver," he responded quickly. "I have always been short off the tee. I've felt the need to gain some distance to be competitive on the Senior Tour and have been making changes to try to gain yardage. But it seems the more I work on it, the worse it gets."

We talked about this. Dave recognized that by thinking of distance when he hit his tee shots, he was swinging harder and faster, resulting in less distance and less control. This in fact eroded confidence in his tee shots, leading to more tension and poorer swings. He agreed that he could break the cycle by deciding at that moment to make consistency and confidence more important than distance. He would try to relax and hit his tee shots with a smooth, consistent tempo. He would forget about distance altogether.

Because his personal confidence was strong, Dave confirmed that he seldom degraded or criticized himself during his rounds. He was not likely to judge himself by his play nor to let a bad round ruin his day.

SELF-SUFFICIENCY

Golf requires skill at making decisions and committing to the decisions you make. In fact, the persistent challenge of decision-making draws many people to this challenging sport. Champion golfers scored well above average on this trait—as did Dave Stockton.

I explained to Dave that we have seen golfers of all levels lower their scores simply by challenging themselves to get fully committed to every shot and putt before they hit them. All golfers we've studied agreed that being committed to the wrong shot would typically give them better results than being uncommitted to the right shot. This acknowledgment often makes it easier for them to trust their first impressions—their instincts—and reduce second-guessing.

Through our discussion, the correlation became apparent between Dave's decision-making and his scores. It also became apparent that Dave understood the importance of commitment to those decisions as we reviewed his play at Crooked Stick. Looking at his round, Dave recognized that, when hitting many of his bad shots, he was to some degree indecisive. He questioned his club, his target, his line. Occasionally, he questioned the type of shot he was trying to hit. Results were usually the same: a poorly executed shot.

Dave agreed to the goal of being fully committed to every shot and putt before execution. Though it is not humanly possible to be 100 percent successful with this goal, he would strive to back off and start his routine again when he found himself addressing the ball with any kind of indecision in his mind.

Competitive golf can be particularly difficult for indecisive or group-oriented people, those who prefer to consult with others when making decisions. It is especially tough for those who prefer that others make their decisions for them. Dave explained that even though he likes to make his own decisions, sometimes the pressure of a very competitive situation makes it too hard to keep up with changing conditions, yardages, difficult lies, ideal targets, and so forth on his own. For this reason, he employs a caddie who is intelligent and keenly aware of what is going on, someone with whom he can confer when he needs more input. He seeks help only as he needs it, so as to reduce confusion or doubt when it comes to making a commitment to a shot or putt.

Group-oriented and indecisive players, meanwhile, must either learn how to increase their self-sufficiency or adopt a sport that requires fewer decision-making skills than golf.

OPTIMUM AROUSAL

Like a lot of golfers not familiar with the language of sport psychology, Dave gave me a puzzled smile when I stated that there is an optimum level of arousal required for golf. We both laughed. "Not *that* kind of arousal," I said. "We're talking about being somewhere between relaxed and tense for peak performance in golf."

"Thanks for clarifying that," he said, still smiling.

I explained that some sports, like target shooting, require that you be extremely relaxed for competition. If there were a "relaxation scale" of one to ten, one being most relaxed, ten being most tense, then rifle shooting would be a two. Sports that require the adrenaline to be pumping, such as football, would score about an eight. Golf, on the other hand, requires that you remain between a four and a six, getting more relaxed from tee to green to make better use of fine motor skills needed for the short game.

Dave tested to be a six, very well suited to golf. We did not have to discuss techniques to aid in "psyching" himself up for competition. Dave's competitiveness does that for him.

Neither did we have to discuss managing his daily tension, as Dave already handled that through a healthy lifestyle that included numerous relaxing hobbies. We chose instead to discuss how he could monitor his tension in competition, largely through the use of "thought checks" and "body checks."

Reflecting on his first round at Crooked Stick, Dave felt he had probably played with an arousal of around four to six, largely because he had few expectations. His only thoughts were to concentrate on each shot. But during the second round, his expectations, his anticipation, and his calculation of the cut and the fear of missing it made him more anxious, and he probably soared to between a seven and a ten. This, he vowed, he would manage better both before and during future rounds.

By the time we summarized Dave's goals, we both realized we had been talking far longer than we had planned. "This was great!" Dave said. "I would like David and Ronnie [his sons] to take this questionnaire, too. I think it would help them with their own games. You know, I would love to be the first PGA Tour player to have a son or sons also make it on the PGA Tour. I may ask Cathy to take it too, to see how we all compare. Speaking of Cathy, I need to find her. She is probably waiting patiently for me in the club house, wondering where I am. I'd like you to meet her. Do you have a few more minutes?"

Welcoming the opportunity I said, "Sure, I would love to meet her." I told Dave I would get him test packets for the rest of his family and that I'd like him to work on one goal at a time, starting with the mental routine. Dave and I agreed we would talk again within a few weeks to monitor his goals and to discuss his Ryder Cup team.

We proceeded to the clubhouse and found Cathy patiently waiting as Dave had predicted. She was warm, personable, and friendly. I immediately sensed that it was from this relationship that Dave drew a lot of his emotional stability, confidence, and motivation. I looked forward to getting to know the whole family.

In the years since we met, Dave has distinguished himself from many of my other Tour clients not only by being one of the hardest workers, but also by being one of the few who seek assistance before there is a problem. He recognizes before a tournament begins whether he needs to adjust his attitude or improve his concentration, and he calls to discuss and resolve anything. In addition, he has proven to be one of the most motivated and efficient at setting and monitoring goals for himself and sometimes for his family.

I feel fortunate to have had at least some small part in helping Dave be successful competitively and personally. It started with the Ryder Cup victory over Europe at Kiawah Island in South Carolina, then progressed through his many Senior Tour victories, and culminated in the distinction of Dave being the first PGA Tour or Senior PGA Tour player to win more than one million dollars in each of four consecutive years.

Perhaps the most enjoyable aspect of our involvement, however, has been hearing the pride in his voice as he reports the progress of David, Jr.'s PGA Tour career, sometimes relaying the latest standings in their personal contest for "most birdies made on Tour" each week. Or when he explains how Ronnie's knowledge of the game has again helped keep Dave's skills sharp and competitive and how he and Ronnie have again teamed up to play well in the Home Depot Father-Son event.

A particularly satisfying aspect of our association has been seeing Dave master, in high-level competition, the incredible challenge of retaining a sharp focus over the ball and a tough-mindedness about his play—while still showing warmth, friendliness, generosity of time, and a genuine concern for family, friends, fans, charities, and tournament volunteers, as well as other professional and aspiring golfers.

He is an example for us all.

IMPROVING YOUR OWN GAME

While we obviously cannot offer you through this book the individualized assistance as we do Dave Stockton or any of our other clients, it is our goal in the following chapters to assist you in as personalized a way as possible. We will provide you with in-depth explanations of each of the eight champion traits and give you useful, concrete suggestions for improving your game after helping you to estimate your own mental skills.

We provide:

○ Charts for you to compare your personality traits to those of champions.
○ Simple self-tests to help you estimate your strengths and weaknesses relative to these traits.
○ Easy-to-use steps for strengthening each of those champion traits that you need to strengthen.
○ Problem-solving illustrations, which use the actual experiences of numerous well-known touring professionals as well as avid amateur golfers.

Reading the following chapters will increase your awareness of how champion golfers think. This awareness alone can begin the process of enhancing your play and your enjoyment of the game.

For those of you who are more serious golfers, we suggest you take a more active approach. Because there are far more suggestions here than you can reasonably expect to incorporate by simply reading, we suggest the following:

1. To best utilize the information, keep a pencil and highlighter in hand. Take the time to complete the self-tests provided. While they are obviously not as statistically reliable and valid as our full questionnaire, the self-tests will help you identify and set goals for strengthening your mental game.

2. Make note of your goals as you identify them. Read slowly with highlighter in hand, marking areas you most want to strengthen. Write page numbers by your goals and go back to these areas *one at a time* to learn and practice the suggested steps.

You will not only be rewarded with newly found strengths for managing your golf game, but for managing your life as well!

One

Focus

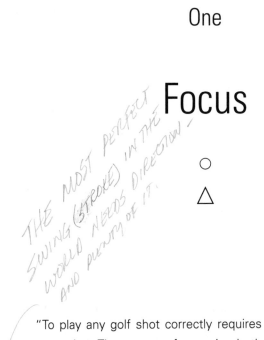

○

△

You might be surprised to discover that the most common
mental problem we encounter when profiling professional
and amateur golfers is "focus"—or rather, an inability to focus.
Yet being able to focus is the foundation of your mental game.

All golfers appreciate the enormous mental discipline required to play the game well, yet so many obstacles and challenges interfere. The irony is that, while these challenges
render the game frustrating and difficult, they also provide the
stimulation and allure that attract so many people to the game
in the first place—not to mention keeping those already playing in constant search of excellence and improvement. Con-
quering golf is to the golfer what the unclimbed mountain is
to the mountaineer.

GOLF'S INHERENT CHALLENGES

Golf is particularly hard on the mind for several reasons.

1. Golf Is Inert

The ball just sits there, waiting for you to make the first move. In momentum sports, such as tennis, you react quickly to the action of a competitor or a ball, and often both. In tennis, your reactive response is to move to the ball and hit it to where your opponent is not. It's much easier to focus when you have to react than when you have time to deliberate.

Golf provides no such momentum to help you narrow your focus. You are left entirely to your own devices to cope with internal and external distractions. If you start thinking about swing mechanics, your score, how other players are playing, how they're scoring, who might be watching you and what they think of your game, you won't give yourself a chance of focusing.

Unfortunately, you are left to your own devices to develop the mental skills necessary to "react" to a stationary ball.

2. Golf Has Too Much "Down Time"

Even when played fast, in four hours or less, golf allows much time between shots for contemplating the game. For many, this is more than enough time to mentally sabotage themselves. Consider the tennis player again, who has little time to do more than react to the next rapidly approaching ball. When you think about it, the only time a tennis player gets to contemplate the stroke is when he or she is about to make the serve.

The golfer, however, has minutes between every shot, and during a round those add up to hours of worrying about the next shot or the holes ahead. A golfer can unwittingly muddy his focus by giving himself swing lessons between shots. He may berate himself for mistakes or concern himself with what others are doing. He might ruminate on the problems in his life off the golf course or worry about hitting his next shot out of bounds. He can easily lose his focus thanks to a variety of random, distracting thoughts.

3. There Seems to Be No Limit on What You Must Do to Hit a Perfect Shot

The more the golfer knows about the game, the worse off he can be. There's that old saying that "a little knowledge is a dangerous thing." Well, that saying especially applies to golf.

During a round, the golfer constantly faces different lies, grasses, grains, inclines, obstacles, winds, and other weather conditions. There are seemingly endless physical variables, including grip, stance, posture, ball position, swing planes, and so on, that must all be in perfect synch for the shot to be executed properly. The golfer must sort through these many details and quickly clear his mind of all but the simplest "swing thought" for the shot at hand. Lack of commitment, and the poor focus that results, can be caused by either underthinking or overthinking these variables. The golfer, in essence, walks a fine line.

4. The Time It Takes to Play a Round of Golf Can Be Mentally and Physically Draining

A round of golf requires four hours or more. So it is vital that the player learns to manage and conserve his mental and physical energies before and, especially, during the round. It is a common problem for a player at any level of the game—from professionals who play many consecutive three- and four-day events to weekend amateurs who spend most of their time working or taking care of the kids—to lose focus because of mental and physical fatigue.

These four factors common to all golfers, along with our own individual mental frailties, make golf one of our most mentally challenging sports.

WHAT IS A CHAMPION GOLFER?

Our study found that players who test above average in terms of being cool and detached, as opposed to warm and outgoing, are best at narrowing their focus over the ball. Curious how you might rate?

What Are Your Tendencies?

Compare your tendencies to those listed in the simple chart on page 39. Keep in mind that 1 represents someone who is extremely cool; 10 represents someone who is extremely warm; and 5 to 6 represents someone who is a combination of the two traits or who is "average" in both. Estimate at which point of the scale you might score on this trait based on *your* personal and golfing tendencies, then circle that number.

The champions either are or have learned to be more on the cool, or focused, side as they prepare to hit their shots and putts.

Players Who Have Cool Personalities

Bruce Crampton, Phil Blackmar, Tom Byrum, and Dave Stockton are all examples of players who tend to be more cool in their personalities. Cool personalities tend to naturally have a more narrow focus and thus a greater power of concentration. Their distractions are typically more internal.

Players Who Have Warm Personalities

Michelle McGann, Paul Azinger, Brad Bryant, and Taylor Smith are examples of players that are especially warm in their

Cool									Warm
1	2	3	4	5	6	7	8	9	10

PERSONAL TENDENCIES:

Prefers more time alone	Prefers more time with others
Internally focused	Externally focused
More introverted tendencies	More extroverted tendencies
Less talkative	More talkative
Reacts to internal stimuli	Reacts more to external stimuli

GOLFING TENDENCIES:

Less aware of partners	More aware of partners
Talks less	Talks more
Less aware of surroundings	More aware of surroundings

personalities. Without extra steps to help narrow their focus over the ball, they can be more easily distracted by activities going on around them. When they are conscious of narrowing their focus over the ball, they can remain fully aware of who is watching, what others are doing, and even carry on conversations, then detach from it all as they "time out" to hit their shots or putts. Paul Azinger is exceptionally good at this when he is playing his best.

INDIVIDUAL CHALLENGES TO "GOOD FOCUS"

Being able to concentrate well is no guarantee you will be able to use such a talent under pressure, particularly if you have one or more of the other personality traits that can interfere with concentration skills—low confidence, high emotions, high tension, indecisiveness, and a tendency to overthink. But whether you have these other inhibiting traits or not, you will improve your ability to focus by learning a strong mental routine. Let's discuss some of these individual challenges to good focus before I share with you the same three-step routine I taught Dave Stockton.

Are you too intelligent to focus? Consider the player exam-

ples listed: Tom Byrum, Bruce Crampton, Phil Blackmar, and
Dave Stockton all have above average abstract-thinking skills.
Each found that the steps recommended in this chapter for
strengthening their mental skills came quite naturally to them,
yet each found it difficult to use them at times because of high
abstract abilities that led to a very "busy" mind. Within seconds of hitting a shot, their minds would be racing away to
their position in a tournament or to all the possible mechanical
variables that went into a shot that may have been hit off-line.
They each showed strong abilities to concentrate, but if they
did not manage their tendency to overthink on the golf course,
they could not maximize their powers of concentration.

Are you too friendly to focus? The extroverted players mentioned, Michelle McGann, Taylor Smith, Brad Bryant, and Paul
Azinger, are apt to notice much more of what is going on
around them and therefore have to work more at eliminating
external distractions to narrow their focus over the ball and
concentrate on the task at hand.

Are you too tense to focus? Some players, no matter how
narrow or wide their focus may be, are more tense than average. Their minds race, and they're far too busy to concentrate
properly. Their focus jumps randomly and quickly to numerous things that do not involve just hitting their shots. Many
pros we profiled, such as Woody Austin, Mark McCumber, and
John Schroeder, are, for various reasons inherent and learned,
more tense.

Are you too relaxed to focus? This is more common in social
golf than in competitive golf, but it also leads to reduced concentration. Golfers who are too relaxed find their minds wandering, doing some of the "mental daisy picking" to which
Bobby Jones refers.

The ability to effectively regulate your focus is the foundation of a strong mental game. Because it is an important
and necessary starting point for players of all levels, we always
teach very simple and reliable skills for managing concentration and focus. From this foundation, other mental skills can

be more easily assessed, taught, and reliably monitored so you can play at your peak more often.

GOLFPSYCH LESSON:
Your Mental Routine

The first step we take, both in private sessions and in workshops, is to assess each player's ability to use a strong mental routine. We then determine how best to enhance it—and we do so by using the single most important performance enhancement technique you will learn.

Using three simple steps, we teach you to willingly regulate your focus.

First, however, we must determine if you already have a mental routine. It's always one of the first questions we ask our new clients. Most respond as Dave Stockton did, saying something like, "Yes, I always set up two inches from the ball and take three good waggles before I look down the fairway, set my feet, and hit my shot."

But that isn't a mental routine. That's a *physical* routine. We then ask about the "mental steps" taken while preparing to execute a shot. Soon the player recognizes that he probably doesn't even have a mental routine. His reasoning? "After it becomes a habit," he'll say, "I can be thinking of just about anything as I prepare to hit my shots." But the golfer shouldn't be thinking just about anything; he should be thinking *only* about hitting the shot.

Our first goal is to initiate a pattern of reliable thoughts that will help you treat every shot the same. The thoughts will clear your mind, relax your body, and help you react to the ball.

The following questionnaire will help you assess the quality of your own mental routine, acquaint you with the basics of a good mental routine, and determine your ability to focus. Using your last round of golf as a measure, answer all of the questions as honestly as possible, applying the following point values. When you've finished, total your scores, and do the math to find out your "mental rating."

1: Always   2: Often   3: Sometimes   4: Seldom   5: Never

3 ___ A. I stepped up to the ball feeling a little unsure about the club and/or the target and/or the type of shot I wanted to hit.

4 ___ B. I stepped up to my putts before feeling completely committed to my line or to my speed.

4 ___ C. I forgot, or it was difficult for me, to stand behind my ball to get a clear picture of the shot or putt I wanted to hit.

3 ___ D. I forgot, or it was difficult for me, to feel the tempo of my swing or stroke as I executed my shots and putts.

3 ___ E. My mind would wander or I was thinking a lot about my swing or the round when I was hitting my shots and putts.

17 _____ Total x 2 ÷ 5 = ___6.4___ Mental Rating

If your mental rating is 8 or higher, your routine and ability to focus during your last round were great. Use this chapter as a resource for understanding your current habits and learning techniques for strengthening them, especially under pressure. If your mental rating is less than 8, then you are just like the majority of our competitive golfing clients were when starting out. Like them, your first mental goal is to develop a strong, three-step mental preshot routine.

GOLFPSYCH TECHNIQUE:
The Three-Step Mental Preshot Routine

Like many players, you may recognize that you already use the following three steps to some degree. But your focus will improve dramatically when you effectively use *all* three steps as part of your whole preshot routine for every shot and putt.

Before reading through the steps, reflect on a shot that

you find to be particularly intimidating or that you frequently miss. Ideally, this shot will be on a hole with which you are very familiar, one that you can easily visualize. Use this shot to mentally practice each step of the routine as you read through it. You may even find it helpful to write down the name of the course, the hole number, the shot, and the particulars of the shot, assuming the conditions and pin placement are where you last saw them.

After each step, take a few moments to relax and practice the *imagery* that is requested. You'll be amazed at how much more effectively you execute your difficult shot the next time you play the hole.

Step 1: Calculations and Commitment

Completing *all* of your analysis of the shot is the first step. This involves gathering all the information—wind, slope, lie, grain, yardage, target, and so on—necessary to make definite decisions about how to hit the shot.

Your focus will begin to narrow as you make a firm commitment to your club, your target, and the type of shot you prefer.

Which club? Pick the club to which you feel you can make a full commitment—one which you have at least a 50 percent probability of successfully hitting, based on the conditions, the type of shot you have chosen, your current physical skills, your level of tension, and the confidence in your physical game at that moment.

What is the target? Choose as definite a target as possible, starting with an area in which you want your ball to come to rest. Then match it with something in the distance—such as a tree or building—that will help you take aim. Intermediate spots or features that are in line with your distant target can be helpful for some players. You must also adjust your target for crossing winds and the shape of the shot you choose.

Which type of shot to hit? Select the type of shot that is ap-

propriate to the situation and within your abilities to successfully execute 50 percent of the time. There may be many options, especially if you are skilled enough to work the ball
confidently. You could choose a draw, a fade, a high shot, a
low shot, a knockdown, and so on.

For putts, the first step of the mental routine is to calculate and commit to two choices.

What is the line? It's the one you choose after you have
considered the length of the putt, the grain of the grass, the
slope of the green, the speed of the green, the wind, and so on.

What is the speed of the putt? Choose the speed you will
roll the ball so that it follows the line you have chosen. You
must consider all the things you assessed when picking the
line. Resist thinking about whether this is a birdie putt or
bogey putt because, except in certain situations, such as match
play or a scramble format, *it does not matter.*

Refuse to make decisions—on any shot—based on what
others are doing or on how the course is "meant" to be played.
Instead, choose only clubs, targets, types of shots, lines, and
speeds that allow you to maximize your skills by fully committing and giving yourself at least a 50 percent chance of executing the shot or putt successfully.

Once you are *fully committed* to all of your choices, you
can move to the second step of the three-step process. If you
find this commitment difficult, remember that you will get
more from your game when committed to the wrong decision
than you will when not committed to the right decision. In
fact, we have had many amateur and professional clients
lower their stroke averages doing nothing more than fully
committing to their decisions—whatever they may be.

> **IMAGERY PRACTICE: Imagine yourself fully committed
> to the club, definite target, and type of shot you want
> to hit on your chosen hole before proceeding with your
> routine.**

Step 2: Visualization

To further narrow your focus and to encourage reactive rather than analytical play, take a brief moment behind the ball—making sure that you are very relaxed—to clearly *visualize* the shot or putt to which you have committed. Visualization ranges from a general impression of the desired ball flight to a very clear mental picture of the flight and landing.

If you are putting, try to see your line from the ball to the hole. This is far easier for "feel" players than it is for "mechanical" players, but the effort enhances the performance of both. Mechanical players will want to find a spot on this imaginary line over which to roll the ball. Imaginative players will prefer to see the entire line. Either works, so long as you have a clear picture of what you want the ball to do.

If you find visualization difficult or if negative thoughts interfere, you probably need to take another deep breath and fully relax your body, then try again. This step of your routine will later serve as a great signal for letting you know when you are overly tense or fatigued.

> **IMAGERY PRACTICE: See yourself behind the ball, fully relaxed, with the club or putter in hand. Try to get a good picture of the ball flight and landing of the shot you chose. If negative thoughts or second-guessing interfere, repeat the process until they disappear.**

Step 3: Feel

In order to further narrow your focus and to promote reactive play, it is important to clearly *feel* the swing or stroke to which you have committed.

Either when behind the ball or beside the ball, try to feel your swing with a good waggle, a partial swing, or, preferably, a smooth full swing. Your goal is to incorporate *one simple swing thought* that allows you to feel the swing to which you have committed. The best swing thoughts tend to be the simplest and are most likely to center on the feel and tempo of your swing. "Smooth back, smooth through," "inside back, smooth through," "tempo," and so on are some swing thoughts that you might use. As you execute your shot, repeat this feel using your swing thought.

When putting, take a practice stroke to feel the rhythm of your stroke. As with a full shot, this may be done either behind or beside the ball. If you have trouble feeling your stroke, relax, take a few deep breaths, and practice your stroke either with your eyes closed or while looking at the hole. You can also try giving your stroke a simple rhythmical count, such as "one back, two through."

As you execute the putt, your emphasis should be on the rhythm of your stroke or the smooth roll of the ball down your intended line and *not* on the importance of making the putt.

> IMAGERY PRACTICE: Imagine yourself behind (or beside) your ball for the purpose of taking a nice full practice swing or a partial swing or a waggle— whichever is most likely to help you truly feel the swing you've committed to use. Once set up, imagine feeling the tempo or the simple swing thought that you've chosen. Imagine executing the shot while concentrating on this same feel.

HOW TO INCORPORATE YOUR MENTAL ROUTINE

Experiment with your mental routine during your next practice session and adapt it so that it complements your physical routine. For example, if you typically take your practice swing behind the ball, you can interchange steps 2 and 3. Do whatever order works for you, *but* we recommend you remain consistent with whatever order you choose. Players who tend to get mechanical over the ball usually find it more effective to make visualization the last step.

The swing thought you choose should be whatever feels good to you on any given day, though we strongly suggest it be as feel-oriented as possible. Rather than thinking of body or club positions, try to feel something in a particular part of your body. For example: After preparing for the 1996 U.S. Open with his swing coach, Lee Janzen found himself thinking far too much about mechanics when he was addressing the ball. So he condensed his lessons into a simple feel—that of keeping his left arm closer to his body. His swing thought for the week became "left close, smooth through." Regardless of the pressure he felt on any given shot, coming back to his swing thought helped keep his mind clear and his play more reactive.

You should settle on one swing thought while you warm up and stay committed to it for at least an entire round. You can even write down those you like and refer to them on days when you find yourself searching.

Your ultimate goal is to treat every shot the same by using the same mental routine for every shot and putt. You should challenge yourself—because it may not come easy—to use the same routine for two-foot putts or twenty-footers, on easy par fives and tough par fours, on sand shots or simple chips, on the first and the last shot of the day (and all those in between), and against easy and tough competitors. Not a single situation should move you away from your mental routine.

Make note when your routine was weak or nonexistent, which you will typically recognize on shots or putts you executed poorly. Once identified, challenge yourself to hit these shots making your routine more important than the actual results of the shot.

In other words, *let the results happen.*

It is very important to practice your mental routine just as you would any other part of your game. On the practice tee, choose a target that closely resembles one you would use for a particularly difficult shot on the course you will be playing. Go through all the steps of your routine, just as you would during a round. This practice is especially important for players with a naturally wider, external focus or for any player who has a pattern of playing several holes before settling into a round.

You should warm up your mental routine as much as you do your swing. This can be accomplished in several ways:

○ Use your full routine on every fifth ball you hit on the practice tee.
○ Take at least ten minutes of your warm-up to "create" various shots on the practice tee or around and on the greens.
○ Use mental rehearsal to play every shot for the first several holes on the range, choosing targets, committing to clubs, visualizing shots, feeling swing thoughts.

Your routine also becomes a much more effective tool if, after each round, you assess how well you used it. A few accompanying notes about circumstances such as your mood, the conditions, playing partners, the significance of the round, will give you great insight to your tendencies and when you must make a concerted effort to use your routine.

A good mental routine accomplishes several important goals. It allows you to play more intuitively, as opposed to manufacturing a swing. It also helps to displace irrelevant thoughts, allowing you to think only about the task at hand. This serves to quiet the mind and relax the body, which, of course, enhances your play. The mental routine helps you make good decisions and helps you commit fully to the club in your hand, your target, and the shot you want to hit, thereby maximizing your physical skills. It also gives you the power of "self-fulfilling prophesy," which, simply put, is the ability to increase the odds of hitting the shot you want by first imagining you will.

WHAT ARE THE SIGNS OF POOR FOCUS?

"I play the tough holes better than the easy ones."

Don't you hear that sort of comment from an awful lot of golfers? Many players notice that they hit better shots on tight fairways and through small openings or that they make more of the difficult putts than the easy ones. What's actually happening is that, without the golfers knowing it, the tougher circumstances are either lowering expectations and narrowing focus to targets, clubs, and types of shots or they are encouraging the golfers to get good pictures of the shots or putts they're about to hit. No wonder they're doing better. Without realizing it, they're doing things right!

Most golfers have inconsistent focus. They are not controlling their focus and are throwing strokes away because they are not treating all shots on every hole the same. No matter what the circumstance, always give each shot the same mental routine and focus.

"I always seem to 'choke' when I'm playing well or when it really means something."

Many players have what some call a "comfort zone." When they find themselves in position to shoot an all-time low score, in contention, or in a position to win a bet, their play quickly goes from great to terrible. Increased tension and emotions can wreck the focus and the fun. But strong and practiced routines serve as "anchors," giving them reliable thought processes that will relax them and allow them to treat every shot the same regardless of its *perceived* importance.

"Before the round is over, I'm exhausted. I feel like I'm working too hard out there."

As we stated earlier, many players—especially the very intelligent ones—tend to overthink and overwork on the golf course. It's not unusual for them to unknowingly play an entire round of golf very mechanically and analytically. They never stop analyzing their mechanics, what they need to shoot, how they'll play holes ahead, or why they missed previous shots or putts. They never release their trained and natural skills by visualizing, feeling, and reacting to their shots. When encouraged to trust their skills by visualizing and feeling, their first response is, "I feel like I'm not trying hard enough!" But if they remain committed to the full routine long enough, golf begins to feel more like a game than a job. Play improves and they finish their rounds with much more energy and enthusiasm.

While using a good mental routine may sound easy, it takes discipline, practice, and patience to use one consistently and effectively. A strong mental routine represents one of the most distinctive differences between champion golfers and average golfers, on both the amateur and professional levels. In fact, the strength and consistency of your mental routine will determine your success as a competitive golfer.

PERSONALIZATION:
Michelle McGann

We are most successful in our work when we can help golfers identify precisely what in their own personalities or habits is inhibiting their ability to effectively use their mental routine. We then recommend specific, personalized steps for strengthening the other parts of their personalities that are sabotaging their ability to focus. The results? Much better play and much more fun.

Let's take Michelle McGann, one of the best players on the LPGA Tour, as a case study of this. Michelle, who is the oldest child and only daughter of Bucky and Bernadette Mc-Gann, began playing golf at the age of seven. She turned professional at eighteen, just after graduating from the Rosarian Academy in West Palm Beach, Florida. In spite of having been diagnosed with diabetes at the age of thirteen, Michelle excelled in golf and was a Florida State Junior Champion three times. Many predicted great things from this long-hitting young lady.

Michelle's parents were just as committed to supporting her as an LPGA professional as they'd been during her amateur career. To help ease the enormous transition and to ensure that someone helpful was around should she experience insulin shock, Bucky became Michelle's frequent caddie and travel companion. Mom and younger brother J.C. joined them both on Tour whenever possible.

With Bucky caddying part-time, Michelle finished 130th and ninety-eighth on the LPGA money list in 1989 and 1990, her first two years on Tour. In 1991, Bucky gave up his landscape and gardening business to join Michelle full-time, largely out of concern for her health. He remained with her from 1991 through 1994, during which time she finished fortieth, eighteenth, twelfth, and sixteenth on the money list. Michelle had established herself as one of the leading players on the LPGA Tour at a very young age. She'd played in more than 150 events, with earnings near one million dollars.

But there was a problem. At five foot eleven inches, and with great "presence," Michelle was easily recognized by her good looks, long drives, stylish clothes, and cheery disposition. She came to be identified by the media as a charismatic player. Still, at the time, she was one of only two players who had won nearly a million dollars in prize money but had yet to win a tournament.

Many around her felt she was more than capable of winning, including Dave Stockton, an early mentor of Michelle's and someone she credits, along with her parents, as having strongly influenced her career. In the spring of 1994, Dave and Michelle had occasion to talk about her game. She told Dave of her frustration with a pattern of bad starts: She would play poorly the first day or two of an event before really settling in to play up to what she, and others, considered her potential. It was almost as if she first had to have a bad round before she could have a good one.

Dave asked Michelle if she was doing anything to strengthen her mental game. She wasn't. He encouraged Michelle to call me.

We spoke via telephone that same week. Michelle described feeling confused about when and how to focus. "It's hard to keep my concentration for all eighteen holes," she said. "I don't want to be serious all the time—and being serious helps, but at the same time doesn't help. Besides, being serious is just not much fun. I like to talk to the gallery and sometimes to other players."

She also acknowledged that at times she did not give her shots enough thought before hitting. "I need to learn not to hit so quickly, to think more about what I am doing," she said.

I asked Michelle to begin by taking the personality questionnaire so we could compare her scores to our champion profile. She explained she was at an LPGA event in Georgia at the time but would be home in Florida the following week. I mailed the test packet to her in Georgia, in time for her to fax her responses to me so I could get the results back to her for review during her off week.

When we next spoke on the telephone, Michelle's warmth and enthusiasm was obvious. She chatted easily and enthusiastically about family, friends, and golf, and I could understand why her personality had endeared her to fans and the media. Yet I knew it also could make focusing and decision-making difficult. As we began reviewing her scores, the profile confirmed Michelle's people-oriented, extroverted style—indicating that she naturally has a moderately wide focus. This makes it easy for her to socialize with playing and pro-am partners, which is good, so long as Michelle can narrow her focus again before hitting the next shot.

I explained that it is important, especially for an extrovert, to allow her focus to open and relax between shots, much as she was doing, using small talk, casual involvement with others, and daydreams. As she approaches her ball, however, she should find a "cue" she could use to signify an exact time to begin narrowing her focus for the shot at hand. Many good players find it helpful to use a simple, physical movement such as opening and closing a glove. Or else they'll give themselves a starting signal—tap a thumb to a forefinger, perhaps, or tap the club on the ground. Some lift and stretch their arms or touch the bill of their hat or simply take the club in one hand.

I suggested that if she watched other pros for their cues, she might see Fred Couples lightly tug on a shirtsleeve, Paul Azinger toss grass into the air (even when there is no wind), or Jack Nicklaus taking a deep breath. Many great players, such as Lee Janzen, begin narrowing their focus with a cue as simple as approaching their ball or opening a yardage book. The more difficulty a player has concentrating, the more unique and distinct they make their trigger. One of our most distracted players found success by starting his routine by snapping a rubber band he had placed on his wrist specifically for that purpose.

We continued our discussion, looking for patterns in Michelle's tournament play. In her early rounds, Michelle was playing only moderately focused. She sounded as though she often hit shots with little forethought, while her mind was still on subjects having little to do with executing the shot at hand. After a few bad holes, Michelle would feel frustrated with herself for not getting more out of her game. She would then try to force shots and opportunities, making it more difficult to perform. Finally, after one or two mediocre rounds, Michelle would feel the challenge of "catching up" with the leaders, still believing her game was good enough to compete with them. This subconsciously motivated her to improve her focus, which improved her play considerably. But even though she might finish well, the damage had already been done.

We reviewed other aspects of her personality that might either enhance or detract from her exceptional skills as a golfer. On the positive side, Michelle's scores indicated a strong ability to think her way around the golf course. She wasted little mental energy overthinking or overanalyzing her game or the surrounding circumstances. In fact, if anything, she actually needed to spend a little more time making decisions about clubs, targets, and types of shots.

She tested to be very competitive, fully capable of challenging a golf course. Being slightly on the dominant side, she was more likely than average to take the calculated risks necessary to maximize her length off the tee, more likely to play too aggressively than to play too tentatively, and at times more likely to impulsively try to force an opportunity, rather than assess the strategy for the best play.

Michelle also tested to have above average drive and motivation, which has a lot to do with her success at such an early age. Professional golf requires both for long-term success. But high drive can be correlated with high levels of tension, and players with too much tension can sabotage their mental play with busy minds that might inhibit good focus. And they can sabotage their physical play with tense bodies, which changes their tempos and fundamentals.

As we completed our discussion, Michelle and I agreed that her primary goal was to strengthen her focus with a strong mental routine. The simple three-step routine I asked Michelle to incorporate into her game is one that has proven effective with both amateur and professional golfers. It is the one you have read in this chapter. It accomplishes all three important goals and, when used consistently and effectively, *always* enhances performance.

To make sure she understood the mental routine, I asked Michelle to select one of her most difficult shots on a hole familiar to her. She was to use imagery to play this shot, visualizing each step of the routine as it was discussed. Michelle chose to use the routine in the described sequence. She made two agreements with herself: If she got over the ball and found that she was not fully committed, she would back off and start the routine again, and if she had trouble visualizing her shot, she would use this as a signal that she needed to take a deep breath and relax, then attempt her visualization again.

To feel her swing, she chose to use the waggle with a swing feel of "pushing back" along the ground in the first six inches of her backswing. (Her favorite swing thought, however, eventually became: "feel a smooth, full turn.")

We determined that it would further help Michelle's focus and her commitment to shots and putts if she would take more time for the first step of her routine—calculating the shot and committing to it. This would be accomplished by taking more responsibility for making decisions on the golf course.

In a conversation I had with Bucky, he indicated he'd already been trying to encourage Michelle to make more of her own decisions and to take more time doing so. He'd simply noticed that her focus was better and she was more committed to her shots when she did this. We all agreed she should do more course management, get more yardages, choose more clubs, and read more putts on her own. All these efforts would get Michelle more mentally involved with her routine. This was to be one of the most important changes she made.

There was a bonus: Her routine served to calm her and slow her down in situations where she would usually rush a shot or putt, such as when she experienced the excitement of good play or the frustration of feeling she needed to make up a lost stroke.

We also found in a later conversation that because of her competitive drive, tension, and excitability, it was important that Michelle breathe deeply between shots as well as during her routine, especially in events where expectations were high or if she had a chance to win. I encouraged Michelle to further manage her tension by learning to regulate her thoughts between shots, and she found that it was easiest to avoid distracting and inhibiting thoughts if she encouraged herself to engage others in light conversation. As she began regulating her thoughts, she found it easier to manage her emotions between shots, which also helped to improve her concentration over the ball.

Michelle remained committed to working on her mental

game, calling periodically throughout the year to discuss problems as they arose. Her focus continued to improve and her routine grew more consistent as she put more effort into decision-making and managing tension on the course. She finished the year with a career-low scoring average of 71.43, seven top-ten finishes, and a second-place finish at the du Maurier Ltd. Classic, one of the LPGA Tour's four major championships. Still, she hadn't won.

In April 1995, having not talked to Michelle for several months, I saw her at an LPGA event in Pinehurst, North Carolina. "I've been meaning to call you," she said. "Do you have some time?" We met after a practice round, and Michelle immediately expressed great frustration and disappointment with not being able to use the mental skills she had worked so hard to attain, especially during one of her most anticipated events, that year's Dinah Shore (another LPGA major). She described feeling easily agitated, impatient, and distracted for most of that week.

"I was hearing every noise around me," she told me. "I was more easily irritated than usual. And I found out at the end of the week that all my clubs were two degrees flat!"

I asked Michelle to help me identify everything else that could be contributing to her feeling so unsettled. "I've been tired and frustrated," she explained, "which has caused my diabetes to be somewhat out of control."

It became apparent that Michelle was feeling stress in numerous areas in both her personal and professional lives. Probably the greatest strain came from some personal conflicts, one of which was her feeling torn about wanting to hire a professional caddie. She wanted golf and family to be separate, she told me, so she could fully enjoy her dad as a loving and supportive father without the distraction of the dual role. But she also did not want him to feel left out.

Michelle needed to simplify her life and reduce her stress, starting with discussing her concerns with her dad. Much to her relief, he clearly understood her decision and supported it, suggesting that it would help her become self-sufficient.

She also recognized that too much of her time and energy was going toward her endorsement contracts and that she needed to manage her time more effectively. That would give her more time to clear her mind and relax both during and between tournaments.

Finally, she needed to rebuild the confidence in her swing that was lost due to the faulty lofts in her clubs. She agreed to get away from tinkering with swing mechanics during her tournament that week and instead put her energies into re-establishing her strong mental routine for every shot.

Success was immediate, as Michelle improved her patience and concentration daily. She went on to shoot 67 during her last round, almost putting her in a playoff. Three weeks later she claimed her first LPGA title with a one-stroke victory over Laura Davies at the Sara Lee Classic in Nashville, Tennessee.

Focus proved to be one of the missing key ingredients for Michelle's success.

Two

Abstract Thinking

○

△

"It's easy for all of us to get too analytical in our approach to golf, and then we wind up taking twice as long to work our way out of a slump than if we'd just let it work itself out naturally."

Larry Nelson, *Golf World*, Feb. 17, 1995

The second of the eight personality traits of champion golfers—abstract thinking—is different from the others in that it is not a measure of temperament. It is a measure of ability. *Abstract thinking is a golfer's ability to analytically reason, problem-solve, learn, and adapt intellectually.* That said, it is affected by traits involving temperament, because all of the eight traits are part of an overall formula.

A golfer who scores high in abstract thinking generally is a fast learner who processes complex information rapidly. This is not always good for golf, however. Abstract thinkers sometimes process so much information that they overwhelm themselves by overcomplicating or overanalyzing swing problems as they try to fix mechanical flaws. This prevents them from playing intuitively. As a result, they lose confidence and find themselves stuck between an old swing they can't get back to and a new swing they can't master.

Someone who is lower on the abstract thinking scale is referred to as a "concrete" thinker. A concrete thinker will tend to be a slower and more deliberate learner, processing information more simply and directly, sometimes oblivious to the many techniques available to improve play. These techniques can be physical and mental, such as adjusting for a sidehill lie or neglecting to change a game plan should the wind shift.

Because abstract thinking is an ability greatly influenced by genetics, we do not expect to increase or decrease the abstract thinking of our clients. Rather, we teach golfers to use their abilities to their greatest advantage. If a player scores high on the abstract-thinking scale, we can safely assume he will need to learn techniques for simplifying his thoughts and quieting his mind over the ball. If a player scores lower on the abstract-thinking scale, we will likely need to encourage him to take more time to preplan his strategy, target, and club selection. Again, we can't influence the basic abstract skills with which he was born, but we can teach him to maximize his inherent skills with planning and effort.

Players at both ends of the scale improve by learning to channel more of their mental energy away from outcome-oriented thoughts—such as score, position, or simple but excessive concern about where a ball might go—and toward the process of their play.

THE ABSTRACT-THINKING SKILLS OF CHAMPIONS

As implied, players at the high and low ends of the abstract-thinking scale tend to sabotage their own play, but because such thinking comes naturally to them, they are generally unaware of the mistakes they make.

The players who think most like champions, on the other hand, are average to high-average abstract thinkers who are skilled at using their ability in ways most appropriate to golf. They avoid problems brought on by overthinking the mechanics and fundamentals of the game. They are also less likely to succumb to underthinking a given situation, such as neglecting to consider all the variables when deciding on club, target, and type of shot. They compete with natural and trained abilities rather than getting immersed in mechanics and fundamentals. They think through a strategy for playing any given course that gets the most from their abilities. They quickly assess and overcome problems so they can put positive mental energy into the shot at hand. And, they usually channel their attention toward a quality routine for the next shot. This makes them consistently good at simplifying their thoughts over the ball and at managing their thoughts between shots.

A good abstract thinker probably has an easier time determining good strategy for playing a course. They understand the variables involved with shot selection (club lengths, lofts, yardages, wind direction and strength, firmness of greens, differing lies, and so on). This enables them to commit to clubs, targets, and types of shots. They also understand the "cause and effect" of shot-making. They know that if their ball is going left, for example, they should first check their mental routine—especially their commitment to the shot and the tempo of their swing—and then check mechanical variables like grip, stance, and ball position.

If you do not naturally have champion abstract abilities, you are not doomed to play frustrating (excessive abstract thinkers) or lackluster (excessive concrete thinkers) golf. You can learn the simple mental skills that have helped golfers of all levels and that can help you play better and more enjoyable golf. The skills include:

○ Recognizing tendencies to underthink or overthink while competing and while preparing for competition.

○ Learning simple methods for getting the most out of your abstract abilities while playing.

What Are Your Tendencies?

Compare your tendencies to those listed in this simple chart. Keep in mind that 1 represents someone who is an extremely concrete thinker; 10 represents someone who is an extremely abstract thinker; and 5 to 6 represents someone who is moderately abstract in his thinking. Estimate at which point of the scale you might score on this trait based on *your* personal and golfing tendencies, then circle that number.

Concrete Thinking							Abstract Thinking		
1	2	3	4	5	6	7	8	9	10

PERSONAL TENDENCIES:

Methodical learner	Fast learner
Linear thinker	Analytical thinker
Likely to underthink problems	Likely to overthink problems
Tendency to simplify	Tendency to complicate

GOLFING TENDENCIES:

Under-reads greens	Over-reads greens
Little thought of "cause and effect"	Too much thought of "cause and effect"
Underplans strategy for play	Overplans strategy for play
Underanalyzes mistakes	Overanalyzes mistakes
Underthinks shots and putts	Overthinks shots and putts
Underlearns the swing	Overlearns the swing

Note: Competitive golf can be an especially challenging sport for players who score at either extreme of this scale.

The champions either are or are striving to balance themselves so that they are only moderately abstract on the course.

Players Who Are Concrete Thinkers

We are not aware of extreme concrete thinkers who have been able to keep their Tour playing privileges.

Players Who Are High Abstract Thinkers

Katie Peterson, Lee Janzen, Dave Stockton, Paul Azinger, JC Anderson, Phil Blackmar, Mark Calcavecchia, Mike Hulbert, Nanci Bowen, and Brad Fabel are all players that score higher on abstract thinking. Each must take steps to simplify their thoughts and quiet their minds during competition, particularly over the ball.

THE DIFFICULTIES INVOLVED IN MANAGING YOUR THOUGHTS

Even with great abstract-thinking skills, managing your thoughts while playing competitive golf can be difficult for those with other particular personality traits, temperaments, and habits. But the overall formula can be improved as long as you are aware of the problem areas and are prepared to work on them. Here are some obstacles that lie in the way of good abstract thinking and some solutions.

Lack of discipline: If you are one of the many people who tend to procrastinate or be unorganized, you may not be making good use of your abstract abilities while on the golf course. Before teeing off, take time to think through at least a basic plan for playing the course. During competition, don't estimate yardages so much—instead walk them off—but do estimate conditions more often; in other words, take more time to assess such factors as wind strength and direction and the direction in which the grain on a green may be running. This is all part of course management, and you'll find more course management suggestions later in this chapter.

Tension: There is not a single champion trait that is not affected by tension. A golfer compromises his abstract abilities when tension causes his mind to race and his mind becomes cluttered with thoughts having little or nothing to do with the execution of the shot at hand.

Lack of confidence: Low confidence leaves a player with poor trust in his abstract-thinking abilities, regardless of how good they may be. This, of course, leads to a lack of commitment, poor play, and a lot of second-guessing.

Emotions: As a player gets more emotional, he naturally gets *less* rational. Instead of using his good abstract abilities, the player is more prone to make decisions by reacting emotionally rather than rationally. We want the golfer to be more methodical when calculating what shot to hit. Thereafter, visualization and feel are important in helping the player react rationally or intuitively to the shot.

A "group" mentality: Some players—especially those who are heavily coached—come to the game conditioned to be more group-oriented than self-sufficient. Their good abstract abilities can be compromised until they practice making their own decisions, especially difficult ones, under the pressure of play.

Other factors: The obvious ones—drugs, alcohol, fatigue, illness, and personal conflict—will muddle your thinking no matter how focused or committed you think you are.

If you feel your abstract abilities are weak, strong, or underutilized, for any of the reasons mentioned above, you'll benefit from learning skills to improve them for competitive golf. The first step is to assess some of your current tendencies while competing, and come up with a mental rating. To do so, simply apply scores to each of the statements below.

1: Always   2: Often   3: Sometimes   4: Seldom   5: Never

___ A. I begin competitive rounds without a well-planned strategy for playing the course.

___ B. I change my strategy for playing the course depending on my score or the strategy of my playing partners.

___ C. I go through a checklist of fundamentals or mechanical thoughts as I prepare to hit a shot or putt.

___ D. After a bad shot or putt, the first thing I do is analyze the mechanical flaws.

___ E. I stay very aware of my score and standing during the round.

___ F. I look ahead in the round with anticipation, fear, or dread of holes yet to be played.

_____ Total x 2 ÷ 6 = _____ Mental Rating

If you rated yourself 8 or higher you likely are making good use of your abstract skills effectively when you compete. If your mental rating was lower than 8, you should seriously consider learning and incorporating the following techniques to maximize your effectiveness in thinking your way around the course.

GOLFPSYCH TECHNIQUE:
Basic Preparation for Both
Concrete and Abstract Thinkers

This helps the concrete thinker be better prepared and helps the abstract thinker simplify thoughts. It involves taking time to preplan your rounds and to monitor your golfing strengths and weaknesses.

Write down a basic plan for playing the course before you hit your first shot. With your knowledge of the course, your score card, and any other available information, decide on a strategy for playing the course that will help you get the *most* out of your game.

o List the clubs and shots you currently feel are your strongest.

o Develop a plan for each hole, starting on the green.

The plan you come up with should reflect your current skills rather than how someone else would play the hole or how you perceive the hole is designed to be played. Starting with the first hole, divide the green into quadrants of four logical parts. Choose the quadrant(s) you can use as a target that will give you more reward than risk. Working backward, choose a position in the fairway—or on the tee of a par three—that will give you your best shot into the quadrant. Select the club and type of shot you would ideally use from that target assuming the most likely conditions. Repeat this exercise until you are back on the tee. Your target and club selection on the tee will now be based on your strategy for playing the hole. You might be surprised to find how often you determine that the driver is not the club to hit from the tee.

GOLFPSYCH TECHNIQUE:
Managing Your Thoughts

Next to developing a good mental routine, learning to regulate your thoughts between shots is probably the most important performance enhancement technique you can learn, not only because it can help you quiet your mind to play more intuitively but also because it can help you manage your emotions, tensions, and confidence. Regulating your thoughts involves becoming aware of, and replacing, thoughts you have during your round that are sure to cause you to lose strength in your eight champion traits. For example, if you are constantly assessing mechanical flaws between shots, you are likely to be too tired mentally before the end of your round.

Unmanaged thoughts typically raise tension and reduce emotional stability. For example, if you spend time between shots getting frustrated at an earlier mis-hit, you will prevent yourself from preparing properly for the next shot. This will raise tension, cause you to feel an emotion such as anger, and probably encourage you to change your game plan by making it more aggressive. You will become more score- and outcome-oriented. All of these reactions to a mishit shot will detract from your ability and give you less chance of playing like a champion.

The hardest part of learning to manage your thoughts, however, is *becoming aware of them*. Once you can identify the thoughts that hurt your performance, you then can take steps toward stopping them and changing them to thoughts that support your efforts. It sounds easy, but it can be quite a challenge to catch and replace these thoughts before they stir your emotions, raise your tension, and clutter your focus.

Once they realize what thoughts they're searching for, most golfers are surprised by the amount of time they spend during a round practicing "stinking thinking," as PGA Tour professional Brad Fabel calls his negative, critical, mechanical thoughts. We call these, and other performance-inhibiting distractions, "not-allowed thoughts." These are the thoughts that interfere with focus, incite emotions, elevate tension, and reduce confidence. In short, they keep you from using all the champion traits.

Identifying Your Not-Allowed Thoughts

So what are some not-allowed thoughts? Listed below are the most common among our amateur and professional clients. Place a check in the box that represents the frequency you have the thought during a round.

Thinking About Your Score

❏ **Always**   ❏ **Often**   ❏ **Sometimes**   ❏ **Rarely**   ❏ **Never**

This is a preoccupation—not a casual awareness—with your score that keeps you involved with your numbers and position. It can interfere with peaceful focus and your ability to give 100 percent to the shot at hand. After their best rounds, our clients consistently describe having only a vague awareness of their score, mainly because they directed their mental energies toward more productive or calming topics.

Al Geiberger describes being hardly aware of his score during his historical round of 59, shot in the Memphis Classic in 1977. Instead of directing his attention to the gathering crowd and why they were surrounding him, Al remained mentally involved with finding little ways to keep himself cool on a very hot and humid day. He, of course, knew he was playing very well, but he chose not to compute his score. At one point, someone in the gallery felt compelled to tell Al he had a chance of setting a record, but, again, Al chose not to acknowledge his score. He continued to focus on one shot at a time and entertain nongolf thoughts between shots. Near the conclusion of the round, Al had to work harder to stay mentally clear of the excitement that had been building. Only after his final putt dropped did he allow himself to fully acknowledge his feat and take part in celebrating what for two decades was the lowest recorded score in the history of PGA Tour golf.

Holes Ahead of You

❏ **Always**   ❏ **Often**   ❏ **Sometimes**   ❏ **Rarely**   ❏ **Never**

This is anticipating holes not yet played. Whether it is done with fear, dread, or excitement, it is a poor use of mental energies and it compromises your ability to concentrate on your next shot.

Lee Janzen acknowledges that one of the primary reasons he was able to remain calm, focused, and competitive during his last round in the U.S. Open at Baltusrol in 1993 was largely because he refused to let himself look beyond the hole and the shot he was playing. He especially did not allow himself to anticipate winning, and he delayed that emotional impact until after his very last putt. Only then did he allow himself to be overwhelmed by the accomplishment. Lee, of course, won the Open again in 1998, following much the same thought process.

Looking Back on Your Round

❏ **Always**   ❏ **Often**   ❏ **Sometimes**   ❏ **Rarely**   ❏ **Never**

If you do this while you're still in the process of playing your round, nonconstructive thoughts of regret, frustration, disappointment, or faulty fundamentals will only take away from the shot at hand and further sabotage your play. Left unchecked, many players spend far too much time between shots dwelling on their previous play. We encourage players to give themselves a couple of seconds to react to their shot, quickly assess which part of their mental routine they could have done better, and move on. You should not look back on your round until you're finished, at which point you can effectively "debrief" yourself and learn from your mistakes.

It is said that, to prevent himself from looking back in his rounds and distracting himself with analytical, negative, or mechanical thoughts while playing, Ben Hogan would imagine building a brick wall behind him. This imaginary wall helped keep his thoughts 100 percent in the present for every shot. He knew his study of the game was best accomplished after the round and that was when he chose to work on his play. We encourage you to follow Mr. Hogan's example.

Negative Self-Talk

❏ **Always**   ❏ **Often**   ❏ **Sometimes**   ❏ **Rarely**   ❏ **Never**

We've all heard players tell their partners, "You talked yourself into that one." This refers to the habit of being self-critical, dwelling on the worst in your play, berating your mental and physical abilities, placing emphasis on faults and weaknesses, or calling yourself names. All this negativity spirals confidence downward, fosters self-doubt, and inhibits play.

Several years ago, Mark McCumber found himself in a challenging position at the PGA Tour's Quad Cities Open.

With a good performance that week, he was poised to exceed his goals for the year by making the top thirty on the money list and to enjoy all the privileges it brings, including entry into the very lucrative Tour Championship tournament that was little more than a month away. Much to his frustration and disappointment, Mark came to the event with some mechanical flaws in his game. With a tendency to expect a lot of himself, to be very hard on himself when he is not playing his best, and wanting so badly to finish high in the standings, Mark was set up to allow his attitude to sabotage his play. Because of this, one of the mental goals we set for the week was one he had been working on all year: *Find something positive to say to himself after every shot and putt.* If he could not compliment something about his play—even after his worst shots and putts—it was to be about himself. Mark committed to this goal and with the help of his caddie remained focused on the positive. This allowed him to get more relaxed, patient, and peaceful as the week progressed. His positive mental state allowed him to better manage his confidence, focus, emotions, and tension, all of which gave him the best opportunity to get the most out of the game. On Friday evening, Mark commented, "This is the first time I can remember hitting the ball this poorly and still leading the tournament!" He remained committed to his goals and went on to win the event, thereby qualifying for the Tour Championship at the Olympic Club in San Francisco. Armed with a stronger physical game *and* a strong mental game, Mark won that event as well. By eliminating all negative self-talk, he went from one unkind word away from disaster to having the best year of his life.

Mechanical Analysis

❏ **Always**   ❏ **Often**   ❏ **Sometimes**   ❏ **Rarely**   ❏ **Never**

While analyzing how to hit a shot and then how to correct a shot comes naturally to most abstract golfers, it generally does more harm than good when you do it during a round. Analy-

sis compromises your use of natural and trained skills. As a result, the player will find himself putting more mental energy
into making a good golf swing than into intuitively playing
his round.

Dave Stockton is not particularly long off the tee, so he
sometimes gets too mechanical when he feels the need for a
long drive. He found himself in this situation on the final hole
of a Senior PGA Tour event when he held a one-stroke lead
over Bob Murphy. In front of a large gallery and a national
television audience, Dave topped the ball. Instead of reacting
or regressing into more mechanical analysis, Dave paused to
ask himself what he could do better mentally on his next shot.
He decided he could visualize his shot better and use a much
smoother tempo. He then turned to his caddie, Todd Newcomb, and joked about the missed shot, saying that he was
trying to entice Murphy to "lay up" on the hole. Focusing on
his mental goals rather than on swing mechanics, Dave parred
the hole, and won the tournament by one stroke.

Thinking About the Outcome

❏ **Always**   ❏ **Often**   ❏ **Sometimes**   ❏ **Rarely**   ❏ **Never**

In simple terms, this is the habit of concerning yourself more
with the results of your shots than with the process of executing them. Many of my clients and I refer to this potentially all-
consuming type of faulty thinking as the "black hole of the
golfer's universe." Everything about the game seems to unwittingly pull you into a state of being preoccupied with outcome
thoughts. You can be totally engulfed before you even know
you are there. And once you are there in the black hole, it is
virtually impossible to play your best golf.

Most golfers fall into this trap because scores are usually
cumulative over eighteen or more holes. After you've finished
a round, those scores become a permanent history of your
skills. The most frequently asked question among professional

golfers is probably, "What did you shoot?" The most fre-quently asked question among amateurs is probably, "What is your handicap?" You will never get far away from outcome thinking, but to play your best, you must learn to manage it.

Several top touring professionals readily admit to falling victim to outcome thinking. Mark Calcavecchia, Robert Gamez, Brandie Burton, Michelle McGann, Jill Briles-Hinton, and Jim Dent all have found outcome thinking responsible for poor scores on par fives. These are supposed to be a pro's birdie hole. All of these golfers can reach the green in two or have good enough short games to get up and down from just off the green in two. So, obviously, they expect to make four, and they count on these holes to lower their scores. But now, with their thoughts over the ball drawn to making four, difficulties arise.

Before tinkering with their mechanics, these players usu-ally find great results by simply going back to their strong mental routine. For example, as they prepare to hit their tee shots, they choose to think less about distance and more about a good target, a good picture, and a good tempo.

Outcome-thinking is common on the green, too, where too often players want a putt to fall so badly—perhaps they're in a putting slump or not playing well from tee to green—that they think about the result rather than the putt itself. Joey Sin-delar, Skip Kendall, Mike Hulbert, Elaine Crosby, Denise Killeen, Allison Finney, J.C. Snead, and DeWitt Weaver are all very good putters who sometimes find themselves too out-come-oriented when they search for reasons behind a recent decline on the greens. Some unknowingly put more pressure on themselves when they want to capitalize on a streak of great ball-striking. Others feel an urgency to make more putts to compensate for poor ball-striking. In either case, fewer putts drop when golfers start thinking more about making a putt than about making a smooth stroke or a nice roll. Each of these players have improved the quality of their putting by simply concentrating more on seeing their line and feeling their stroke and less on how much they need or want to make the putt.

What Others Think

❏ **Always**   ❏ **Often**   ❏ **Sometimes**   ❏ **Rarely**   ❏ **Never**

Do you concern yourself with the thoughts and opinions of others as you try to compete? You shouldn't because what you're doing is the equivalent of trying to read the minds of other players, the gallery, teachers, coaches, family, or friends in anticipation of their judgment, their disapproval, or letting them down. Such thinking typically clutters focus, elevates tension, increases emotions, and sabotages play.

Nanci Bowen learned near the end of her first year on the LPGA Tour the problems created by being too involved with what others think of her play. The disappointment of possibly not playing well enough to keep her Tour card was difficult enough, but she also felt the tremendous burden of "letting down" those closest to her. Being the youngest in a large and close family, Nanci unknowingly was in a role of wanting to play well for her very supportive parents and siblings. Playing poorly meant having to call home that evening and experience their disappointment too—or so she perceived. She'd find herself dreading the call in the middle of a tournament. She'd ruminate over what she'd have to say and feel its impact—sometimes well before the end of her round. Nanci became aware of the negative influence this kind of thinking had on her play, and she worked to change it. She explained to her parents what she was challenging herself to do. And she decided to reduce the frequency of the calls home—eliminating temptations to plan them while still on the course—and to talk less about her golf when she did call. Her parents readily understood, which made it much easier for her to accomplish her goal of intercepting and replacing all self-conscious thoughts related to her play. Though she lost her LPGA playing privileges that year, she set numerous mental and physical goals for strengthening her mental game. Nanci honed these skills on the Futures Tour and that fall regained her LPGA playing privileges. She later won an LPGA major championship, the Dinah Shore, and remains a prominent LPGA player today.

Identifying Your "Allowed Thoughts"

The next step in regulating your thoughts is to identify positive, constructive, and peaceful thoughts to think about between shots to help edge out the not-allowed thoughts. The logic is similar to that of counting sheep to help you fall asleep. The goal is to displace the stressful thoughts that are keeping you awake with thoughts involved enough to keep you minimally mentally engaged—like counting—and thoughts simple, peaceful, and relaxed enough to keep you at ease—like imagining sheep gliding over a fence. Soon you relax and drift off to sleep.

You can only think of one thing at a time, so that one thing should be something that helps create a mental state suited to what you are trying to do. On the golf course, you should aspire to:

○ remain relaxed and peaceful;
○ clear your mind;
○ imagine what you want to feel and do;
○ give yourself "mental breaks" between shots.

The last objective surprises many golfers. They say, "You mean I'm not supposed to be thinking of my round the whole time I'm out there?" And we say, "Absolutely not. If you do, you will likely finish your round mentally exhausted."

Here are some of the favorite allowed thoughts of a few touring professionals, which are effective for players of all levels. Perhaps they will trigger some ideas of your own.

Fred Couples

Sports, sports, sports: Freddie loves to talk about any and all sports with his caddie, Joe LaCava, another sports nut. Whatever is going on in the sporting world, these two will be talking about it.

Outlining trees. Freddie came up with it but now many of our clients use it. When he is especially nervous or concerned about his round, he looks for the biggest tree in sight and begins outlining it in his mind. He slowly takes his eyes around the entire profile of the tree. When he's finished, his body is relaxed and his mind clear. You can do this with any object, not just a tree. We call this technique "object meditation" and we will explain it further in chapter 8.

Daydreams: All players have their favorites. At various times, Freddie's daydreams have been of gardening, tinkering with cars, playing with his dogs, and lying on his favorite sofa watching TV.

Past great shots: Sometimes when he finds himself fearing an upcoming shot, especially when in contention, Freddie will quickly take a moment to recall the last time he hit a similar shot extremely well. He mentally takes himself through the things he felt and thoughts he had as he hit that shot. Then, as he prepares to hit the shot at hand, he imagines himself in the location of that last great shot doing an exact replay.

Phil Blackmar

Fishing: One of Phil's favorite things to do when he's home in Corpus Christi, Texas, is to fish for redfish in the Gulf of Mexico. So he regulates his thoughts by imagining he's doing just that. Because he is a very abstract thinker, Phil creatively came up with a fun image that could stop his mind from racing and keep his thoughts simple and his body relaxed. He would visualize himself baiting his hook with his not-allowed thoughts and casting them into the gulf.

Once, when he was not hitting the ball well, Phil used

this imagery to make the cut at The Players Championship. I saw him as he made the turn on Friday, and he told me that although he was struggling physically he was keeping himself from dwelling on his mistakes. "Although," he said jokingly, "one of those redfish got so big it broke my line!"

Brad Fabel

Music: Brad lives in Nashville and has more than a few favorite tunes. When he feels his body get tense and his mind race, usually in the heat of competition, Brad softly whistles one of those songs. This helps calm him, clear his mind, and get him back into the rhythm of his play. We've found that many golfers can get rid of not-allowed thoughts by whistling, humming, or just imagining hearing a favorite song as they play. For the sake of your playing partners and their possible wrath, we suggest you keep the volume low.

Steve Veriato

Breathing: Steve, a Senior Tour pro, uses anxiety as a cue to check his thoughts for concerns that are outside his control rather than allowing it to take over his play by making him tense. Let's say he identifies the cause of the anxiety as the possibility of hitting a ball into a water hazard. He uses this as a reminder to take a deep, relaxing breath. Then he thinks about something totally within his control, such as choosing a definite target and feeling a great, smooth tempo as he swings. Steve also finds it relaxing, both physically and mentally, to concentrate on smooth, relaxed breathing when walking the fairway in anticipation of a difficult shot or putt.

Dave Stockton

One of the masters at regulating thoughts, Dave uses many techniques for clearing his mind between shots.

Nature: Dave loves to hunt and fish. While playing tournaments, Dave can frequently be found scanning his surroundings for wildlife that is likely to be found in the area—rabbits, turtles, fish, birds, snakes, and alligators. In locations known to have wild edible berries growing on the course, Dave has been seen scouting for any that are ripe for picking.

Hobbies: Dave always seems to have some fun project or trip in the works, which he frequently reflects on or talks about with his caddie or sometimes other players in his group—particularly during slow rounds. He might be planning a hunting or fishing trip, thinking through work he plans to do at his California orange grove or buffalo ranch, discussing a complex puzzle he is assembling, or planning time for a needlepoint project he volunteered to help complete for a charity auction.

Cathy: Dave's most loyal and devoted fan and coach is his wife, Cathy. She tirelessly walks the courses, gets herself involved with every shot (in a nondistracting way), and provides Dave great "mental breaks" by chatting with him by the gallery ropes.

Jackie Gallagher-Smith

Walking and talking with confidence: Jackie came to recognize that as her self-talk got bad during a competitive round, her shoulders would drop, the rhythm in her movement would change, and she would lose the natural spring in her step. It became her goal to watch for these changes as signs to check her thoughts between shots. Any not-allowed thoughts were to be replaced with walking and talking with confidence, including keeping her shoulders back, her chin up, and moving to her natural rhythm. When she accomplishes her goal, spectators cannot discern her score by her mannerisms.

PERSONALIZATION:
Lee Janzen's Success Story

In concluding this chapter, I'd like to discuss Lee Janzen, at this writing a two-time U.S. Open champion and one of the many great golfers who raised his game another level by simplifying his thoughts over the ball.

Here's what Payne Stewart had to say after playing in the same group as Lee during the 1995 Players Championship, which Lee won: "He always seems to stay calm and not get caught up with the pressure. I mean, we're walking down the eighteenth fairway and he says to me, 'I can't believe [the on-course commentator] Dan Pohl hasn't gotten us the score of the [Orlando] Magic basketball game.' "

Here's what Lee has said about his approach: "After a bad swing, I used to take a bunch of practice swings in between shots, from the tee down to the ball, trying to figure out what went wrong. But now I don't take any of those analytical swings. I just walk up to the ball and try to feel my way to the proper swing."

Clearly Lee has disciplined himself to use his above-average abstract thinking skills as an asset.

Encouraged by his wife, Beverly, Lee contacted us in August 1994 to inquire about taking our personality questionnaire. He already had devoted considerable time to developing his mental skills by using the books, tapes, and seminars of motivational guru Tony Robbins. Although he had learned to become a more positive thinker, he felt he was not getting the most out of his efforts, that somehow he was getting in his own way. He wanted to find out why.

When completing our initial questionnaire, Lee identified his golf strength as "desire" and his golf weakness as the "inability to be in the peak state all the time." His one simple, stated goal was "to be my best every day."

Lee couldn't yet pinpoint why it was happening, but he felt he was "falling off" the great year he had in 1993. He had won the biggest victory of his career in a head-to-head battle with Payne Stewart at the U.S. Open at Baltusrol. He not only won by two strokes, but he tied Jack Nicklaus for the lowest cumulative score in U.S. Open history and became only the second person in a U.S. Open, after Lee Trevino, to post four rounds in the sixties. In the same year he won the Phoenix

Open and finished the season with earnings of $932,335, ranking him seventh on the PGA Tour money list.

When we met in December 1994 to discuss both his profile and his year, I soon realized that it had taken a lot for Lee to ask for the assistance—not only because he is somewhat introverted (more so, he said, since winning the 1993 U.S. Open), but also because he is very self-reliant. Plus, like most players who have recently won a major, his anonymity, privacy, and personal time were all a little harder to come by.

As we reviewed his year, Lee and I noted the more obvious things that might have affected his play. In the first half of the year he had been bothered by a hernia that he had surgery on in July. He was a new father, happily traveling with Beverly and their infant son, Conner. But adjusting to fatherhood and all the challenges that it brings—including not sleeping through the night—made things a bit more difficult on Tour. Adding to his distraction were decisions to change management groups and to change equipment—twice. He had a lot of extraneous things going on.

Lee admitted to feeling little of his usual focus. Of the twenty-six events he played, he estimated that he maintained good, relaxed focus from beginning to end in only two—the Buick Classic and the Kemper Open. The Buick Classic is played at the Westchester Country Club, a course he dearly loves, and he shot 64 and 66 the final two days to finish just ahead of Ernie Els. At the Kemper, another favorite tournament, things again "seemed to fall into place," and he finished fourth. Though he was not sure why, in these two events he felt more at ease, more patient.

As we discussed the differences in how he thought at these tournaments versus the twenty-four others, it became evident that Lee had fallen into playing most of his golf with many mechanical and analytical thoughts. In most of these tournaments, he'd been preoccupied with swing mechanics, scores, money, position, and other distracting topics.

Because Lee tested to be well above average in abstract

thinking, we already knew he was prone to overthink. The thoughts that preoccupied him during many of his rounds only confirmed the need for Lee to regulate his thoughts. He agreed he could do more to improve his attitude for competition, rather than wait for circumstances to do it for him.

He was immediately motivated to begin the use of the three-step mental routine outlined in Chapter 1 to help him use his good concentration skills over the ball and, even more important, to play more by feel. He found it helpful to come to a brief but complete stop behind the ball, giving himself a definite end to the analysis of how to hit the shot and a beginning for the visualization of the shot. It also gave him a moment to fully relax his body, taking a deep breath whenever he found himself tense.

Lee recognized that his preoccupation with mechanical and outcome thoughts was largely driven by recent circumstances: equipment changes, concern about his position on the money list, the responsibility of a new child, the whirlwind of expectations and demands placed on a U.S. Open champion. He vowed to take better control of his thoughts on the course.

Lee quickly learned, through awareness and practice, to catch and manage the not-allowed thoughts. He began 1995 well, winning The Players Championship. He then added the Kemper Open title in June.

Lee also took the concept of managing one's thoughts to an even higher level: He came to anticipate and plan for potentially distracting thoughts even before they became a problem.

One such example occurred before the PGA Championship at Riviera Country Club in Los Angeles in 1995. Lee went into the event with a slim but earnest hope of earning enough points to qualify for that year's Ryder Cup Team. Ten players make the team based on point standings, and qualification looked to be a little far out of reach for Lee, despite his two victories earlier in the year. Still, two other players are picked by the team captain—in this case, Lanny Wadkins—and Lee felt that even if he couldn't accumulate the necessary points, a convincing performance at Riviera would earn him one of those spots. The picks were to be announced later that week.

Lee suggested we meet early in the week to prepare mentally for all the internal and external distractions. Besides a number of stressful business issues that he had to put aside, Lee's major goal for the week was to prepare himself in advance for any performance-inhibiting, not-allowed thoughts that would likely crop up. As we discussed his circumstances, we listed on paper all the obstacles in the way of maintaining a relaxed and peaceful focus. We then sorted through the list and tagged those that were the most likely to interfere and distract. They were principally outcome thoughts related to score, position, points, Wadkins's opinion of his play, and striving for a position on the Ryder Cup Team. After imagining scenarios most likely to trigger these thoughts, such as a bad shot, a bad hole, or comments about the Ryder Cup Team, Lee thought through a simple mental strategy that would deal with each of them.

For example, he chose to minimize any thoughts and discussions about the Ryder Cup. Instead, they would serve as his reminder to get back immediately to his mental goals for the week. We also discussed the challenges he would face *after* the Ryder Cup announcement. He would face questions and comments from both the media and fellow players if he did not make the team. Rather than dread this possibility, we discussed an approach to using even the worst outcome to his advantage. This included viewing these questions and comments not as reminders of his possible disappointment, but, again, as reminders of his mental goals for the week.

Lee remained mentally strong throughout the PGA. One of his best displays came when he aced the par-three sixth after errant play on the par-four fifth. Although he played well, he ended up a few points short of making the team. And to the surprise of many, he was not announced as a captain's choice. Though many questioned Wadkins's decision to pick Curtis Strange over him, Lee took total responsibility and vowed to dedicate himself to making the 1997 team, which he did. Being well prepared for this scenario, Lee was able put his mental goals back in place immediately.

The following week, at The International in Colorado, as anticipated, Lee was inundated with questions from reporters, players, friends, and fans. Again, because he was prepared, these questions not only were cues for him to commit to his mental goals, but they also strengthened his awareness and involvement with those goals. He used preplanned responses to the questions, thereby avoiding becoming too mentally or emotionally involved with the topic. Believing the best reply of all was a strong performance in The International, Lee maintained great mental toughness.

Using his cues effectively and keeping his mental game strong all week, Lee won the tournament, making himself the number-one player on the PGA Tour at that time, both in wins (three) and earnings (nearly $1.3 million).

Three

Emotional Stability

○

△

"In the past, I would've stayed mad for four holes, but that was everything I promised myself I wasn't going to do when I came out on the Senior Tour. About midway through last year [1994], I made up my mind I was just going to play golf and enjoy it."

Bob Murphy, 1995

The above-average ability to stay emotionally uninvolved with results during a round of golf is another one of the traits that distinguishes champions from average golfers. Bob Murphy won four times in 1995 after committing to change his habits and strengthen this part of his personality. Numerous factors besides habits and basic personality—lifestyle, circumstances, and even body chemistry—play a role in making some of us more prone than others to express emotions.

This is not to say that all emotion is bad. Emotions enrich our golf and our lives with meaning, purpose, and passion.

Emotions feed the unrelenting desire to hit a longer drive, a more accurate approach, and a more certain putt. The emotions we plan to address here, however, inhibit performance on the course. These are the emotional extremes—the higher levels of anger, frustration, disappointment, stress, fear, insecurity, and even some of the more positive emotions of excitement, elation, and anticipation as well. Extreme emotions —no matter what part of the emotional spectrum they're on— alter your play by impairing your ability to use your mental and physical skills properly.

Here are examples of how all seven of the other eight traits of champion golfers can be impaired by extreme emotions.

- Focus: Your ability to narrow your focus over the ball is reduced as your emotions elevate, thereby compromising your mental routine.
- Abstract Thinking: Rational allowed thoughts and well-planned strategy are lost to irrational not-allowed thoughts and emotional reaction.
- Dominance: Competitive and moderately aggressive play is made too aggressive by anger or too tentative by fear.
- Tough-Mindedness: The strong, tough, resilient competitor is reduced to one who is sensitive, uncertain, and easily distracted.
- Self-Confidence: Emotions can lead to negative and degrading self-talk, which erodes both self-confidence and confidence in your game.
- Self-Sufficiency: Even good decision-makers have a more difficult time committing to clubs, targets, and types of shots when experiencing extreme anger, fear, frustration, and disappointment.
- Optimum Arousal: Tension levels usually climb as your emotions do; it is difficult to manage one without managing the other.

THE CHAMPION GOLFER

Our champion golfers are above average in emotional stability. They seldom let their emotions climb to a level at which their rational thought and control start to be compromised. However, it's not that they mask or suppress their emotions. Instead, they *understand* their emotions and *manage* them.

Some personalities find it easier to recover from an emotional outburst while others find it easier not to react in the first place. Most of us, though, remain vulnerable to experiencing the emotional roller coaster in our competitive rounds of golf. Let's see where you are on the emotional scale. Review the chart on page 85 to assess how much you may be currently experiencing your emotions.

What Are Your Tendencies?

Compare your tendencies to those listed in this simple chart. Keep in mind that 1 represents someone who is extremely emotionally unstable; 10 represents someone who is extremely emotionally stable; and 5 to 6 represents someone who is a balance between the two. Estimate at which point of the scale you might score on this trait based on your personal and golfing tendencies, then circle that number.

The champions either are or strive to be more emotionally stable. Assess where you might fall on this scale and how much you may be currently experiencing your emotions.

Players Who Experience Their Emotions

Mark Calcaveccia, Robert Gamez, Bruce Leitzke, Craig Stadler, Dottie Pepper, Jim Dent, Bob Murphy, and Maggie Will are examples of players who experience the highs and lows of their emotions more than average. Each has learned to tame and channel their emotions into playing great golf.

Experiences Emotions							Emotionally Stable		
1	2	3	4	5	6	7	8	9	10

PERSONAL TENDENCIES:

Easily frustrated	Seldom frustrated
Quick to anger	Slow to anger
Tends to worry	Usually worry-free
Cries easily	Seldom cries

GOLFING TENDENCIES:

Strong reaction to shots	Little or no reaction to shots
Often angry while playing	Seldom angry while playing
Difficulty forgetting mistakes	Easily recovers from mistakes
Dreads challenges	Accepts challenges
Anxiously anticipates outcome	Peacefully focuses on process

Players Who Are Very Emotionally Stable

Less likely to have to manage highs and lows of emotions are players who are naturally more emotionally stable. This does not make them emotionless, just less likely to sweat the small stuff. These include Brian Claar, Kris Tschetter, Katie Peterson, and Clark Dennis.

CHALLENGES TO GOOD EMOTIONAL STABILITY

We have found that even players who have above average emotional stability can lose their cool when faced with one or more emotion-provoking situation. Let's call those situations challenges. Your ability to manage your emotions will be influenced by your skill at handling the following challenges.

Expectations: "I lost the French Open in 1971, when I was defending champion, because I was unable to control my emotions," wrote David Graham in his book *Winning Golf.* This is an example of how it is common for golfers to record bad rounds when their ball-striking and putting are good. For most, this is a result of conscious or subconscious expectations placed on their games. Expectations become emotional traps, setting the players up for frustration and disappointment.

Expectations do not only concern hitting the ball well. They could be rooted in your playing a course you especially like or have played well before; practicing many long and hard hours; getting physically fit and diet conscious; or a combination of these and other seemingly positive influences. As these influences subtly stir emotions of desire, longing, and anticipation, you become primed for almost instant frustration, disappointment, and anger when your shots aren't hit exactly as you expected, and your scores aren't as low as you hoped.

The best players prepare themselves for the trap of not living up to expectations by making themselves aware of any expectation that can do damage—because acknowledging your expectations softens their impact on your emotions and, therefore, your play. One good exercise is simply to write them down. This will increase your awareness and even allow you to file them away as a symbolic gesture of leaving them at home.

Perfectionism: This personality trait takes expectations to the maximum level. When players go into competition feeling they should hit no less than perfect shots and perfect putts, ball-striking can unwittingly become more important than actually playing the game. With this mindset, players are doomed to experience floods of emotion, at least partially because they have chosen a sport that cannot be perfected. And a perfectionist doing something that cannot be perfected is a classic formula for frustration, anger, and disappointment. It is important to remember that in golf diligent work does not always ensure perfect play.

To compensate, perfectionists must accept less-than-perfect performances, less-than-perfect shots, less-than-perfect results. They must change their attitude about what they should be able to do, and try to do only what they *realistically* can do. Later in this chapter you will see how we help perfectionists accomplish this goal by teaching them two Golf-Psych techniques: "Process vs. Outcome" and "Margins for Error."

Pain: Pain can increase irritability, reduce patience, and elevate negative emotions. Unfortunately, playing with pain, particularly shoulder, hip, and lower-back pain, is a common problem among golfers. But pain can be managed by (1) doing physical exercises (for both prevention and treatment), (2) taking lessons to correct faulty mechanics, and (3) learning mental techniques that minimize the intensity of pain. (While medication can manage pain, we discourage its use without medical supervision or without first trying these three methods of pain management.)

LPGA Tour veteran Kristi Albers competed for many years with moderate to severe lower back pain—one of the most common ailments in golf—to the point that she found it nearly impossible to play without some level of fear, frustration, and disappointment. Taking these three steps helped her to again enjoy competitive golf. "It is easier to play golf without being so emotional," she told me. "My physical therapist gave me exercises to keep my back strong, I found a teacher to correct some of the problems causing the pain, and you helped me learn to relax and minimize the pain."

Mental fatigue: Mental fatigue leaves you with little or no patience, hinders you from making and committing to decisions, and makes managing emotions nearly impossible. Its causes include practicing too much, playing too much, remaining too mentally involved with your round between shots, overanalyzing your play, being out-of-balance in your life away from the course (working too hard, stress, sleep shortages, irregular meals), or any combination of the above.

The first step to avoiding mental fatigue is to recognize that allowing yourself to overanalyze, worry, and experience emotions only prevents you from playing the best golf possible. You must learn to expend your mental energy efficiently. You can do this by taking mental breaks between shots or just finding the time to relax during your round. You should resist wasting mental energy on not-allowed thoughts. Taking care of yourself with proper diet and rest are equally important.

Body chemistry: Each of us has a unique body chemistry that contributes to how much we experience emotion. If you are unable to control your emotions by changing your thinking habits, you should consider checking for biological influences. A good diet, exercise, dietary supplements, and in some cases antidepressant medication can help you gain control over your own emotions when body chemistry is a contributor or cause of your mental stress.

Hypoglycemia and hyperactivity: Both of these physical disorders can make managing emotions extremely difficult, even when you attack them with an arsenal of mental techniques. Hypoglycemia, also referred to as low blood sugar, is caused by an oversecretion of insulin by the pancreas. In addition to emotional instability, other symptoms can include restlessness, fatigue, anxiety, dizziness, headaches, irritability, depression, a craving for sweets, or impaired memory. Golfers with low blood sugar who have not had a healthy meal or snack will often notice sudden drops in concentration and patience. We see these changes in golfers within a few holes of making the turn or about an hour after their last sugary drink or snack.

Reported causes of hypoglycemia are varied but those that are popularly recognized include:

- junk-food diets
- excess dietary sugar
- food allergies
- too much alcohol, caffeine, or nicotine
- stress
- exhausted adrenal glands from prolonged stress
- liver damage
- hypothyroidism
- irregular and large meals

If you think you may be hypoglycemic, ask your doctor for a six-hour glucose tolerance test. (Two- and four-hour tests are also available, but don't always reveal the subtle drops in blood sugar that you may experience during a round of golf.) Holistic health advocates suggest that you:

○ Minimize the use of sugar, refined and processed foods, white flour, soft drinks, salt, caffeine, alcohol, and cigarettes.

○ Balance your intake of food into five smaller meals per day, such as three small but well-balanced healthful meals with two healthful balanced snacks between them.

○ Take steps to reduce the stress in your life and incorporate the relaxation skills we will teach you in Chapter 8.

It is important to try to have a well-balanced meal before playing a round of golf and at least one nutritious snack on the course. These snacks are especially important to the players who are too nervous to eat a full meal before teeing off.

The unpredictability of tee times, the length of some rounds, and the unavailability of healthful food and drink on the course can make managing your blood sugar difficult. Therefore, the hypoglycemic, as well as the diabetic, should carry their own snacks. This has become easier in recent years with the advent of the popular sports nutrition bars. They are easy to carry and are formulated to give you sustained energy; the best products seem to have a good balance of carbohydrates and protein. Many players, however, still prefer putting together their own snacks—fruit, nuts, sandwiches, boiled eggs, trail mix, and protein drinks will all suffice.

A close friend of Al Geiberger, the late Dr. David McMahan, a physician and an avid golfer from San Antonio, Texas, diagnosed Al as hypoglycemic early in his career. While playing in various pro-am rounds with Al, he began noticing fairly consistent and significant changes in Al's energy, concentration, and focus after about two hours of play. Dr. McMahan encouraged Al to start carrying a nutritious snack in his bag to munch on as he played, thereby keeping his blood-sugar up and his mental skills strong. Al found this to be so helpful that, to this day, a traditional part of his weekly preparation is the purchase of peanut butter and bread so he could make sandwiches to eat during his rounds. On tour he is not only known as Mr. 59, but also as Mr. Skippy, in reference to his favorite brand of peanut butter.

Hyperactivity is a disorder related to the central nervous system. Common symptoms may include emotional instability, a quick temper, impatience, poor concentration, high drive, tension, an inability to relax, and sleep disturbances. Common stated causes include mineral deficiencies; amino acid deficiencies; malnutrition from too many refined, sugary junk foods; intolerance to preservatives and additives; hypoglycemia; some prescription drugs; and pesticides. Many think the symptoms are made worse by excessive sugar, caffeine, chocolate, luncheon meats, hot dogs, fats, and fast foods.

If you experience any of the symptoms of hyperactivity, consider the following suggestions:

○ Choose foods wisely, eating fresh, as opposed to packaged and processed, foods whenever possible.
○ Avoid excess caffeine, alcohol, and sugary drinks.
○ Balance your intake of carbohydrates and protein, much like the diet recommended by Dr. Barry Sears in his book *The Zone*.
○ Take daily supplements that (1) help maintain your nervous system, including calcium, magnesium, vitamin E, vitamin C, and vitamin B complex, and/or that (2) regulate neurotransmitters, including various amino acids. Consult with a certified nutritionist to determine supplements that will best meet your needs.
○ Learn skills for managing your time efficiently and include quality time for relaxation.

Suppressed anger and frustration: Unresolved personal issues contribute heavily to emotional instability on the golf course. It's a situation that probably is more common than you think. The death of a loved one, personal or family accidents and illnesses, money pressures, marital strife, and other issues can create emotions that will somehow find their release on the golf course.

Interestingly, players who are good at repressing their feelings sometimes seem to play better when their lives are in chaos, because golf is a temporary escape or release from their problems. But the irony is short-lived. It is usually just a matter of time before the significant issues of their lives come crashing down on them, greatly reducing their ability to compete.

Far better than repressing or suppressing these issues is resolving them as efficiently as possible—not simply because it will improve your handicap but, more important, because it will improve the quality of your life. Resolving issues minimizes unmanageable emotions during the pressures of competition. Counseling can facilitate and speed you through this process.

HOW TO ASSESS YOUR OWN
EMOTIONAL STABILITY

Based on your last competitive round, answer the following six questions, using these numbers. Then do the math.

1: Always   2: Often   3: Sometimes   4: Seldom   5: Never

___ A. I get angry with myself after missing a shot or putt—and still feel it when I hit my next shot or putt.

___ B. A bad round can affect my mood for hours.

___ C. A spectator could determine how well I am playing by watching my mannerisms.

___ D. I dread or fear certain shots or putts.

___ E. After a great shot or hole, my excitement distracts me
      from using a great routine on my next shot.
___ F. I find myself anxious about where my shots or putts may
      go.

_____ Total x 2 ÷ 6 = _____ Mental Rating

If you rated yourself 8 or higher, you likely are emotionally stable
on the golf course. If you rated lower than 8, you should take
steps to understand the source of your emotions, and try to reduce them through appropriate lifestyle and attitudinal changes,
as well as the following two GolfPsych Techniques that we have
found to be most helpful in managing emotions. Both these techniques are important foundations for effectively using these and
other GolfPsych Techniques to strengthen your mental game.

GOLFPSYCH TECHNIQUE:
Process vs. Outcome

"All year I concentrated on 'Forget the last shot.' . . . The only
thing you can control is your attitude toward the next shot."

Mark McCumber, 1994, his best year on Tour

We often point out to our clients that the greatest differences
between champions and average golfers is the way they think.
And one of the biggest differences is rooted in whether the
player is oriented more toward the *outcome* of his play or the
process of his play.

Being outcome-oriented is the more natural approach to
the game. The game itself encourages emphasis on end results,
quality of shots and strokes, perfection, and accomplishment.
We often hear television commentators say "It's not how, it's
how many." Being process-oriented, on the other hand, is
more about "how"—and that comes less naturally to most. It
emphasizes enjoying the game, keeping a quiet and peaceful

mind, and accepting all adversity as a challenge to staying relaxed and focused on hitting one shot at a time.

There are many examples of good players who became
great players by shifting successfully from being outcome-
oriented to being process-oriented. One such player was the
great Bobby Jones, who earlier in his career showed dramatic
displays of emotion and great anger toward himself in response to poor results on the golf course. The first time he
played the Old Course in St. Andrews, Scotland, for example,
he was so befuddled by the strange bumps and bounces of
links golf that he tore up his scorecard and walked off the
course. As he matured, however, Jones was inspired by Harry
Vardon to adopt a different attitude, one acknowledging that
all you can really do is "just keep hitting the ball to the best of
your ability." This shift from being emotionally involved with
the results of his shots, to the challenge of concentrating only
on the shot at hand, helped him tame his emotions and put
his mental energies into the process of his play. He soon became one of the greatest golfers in history, and winner of several championships at St. Andrews.

Dave Stockton is a modern-day player who plays his best
when he keeps his objectives simple. He sometimes reinforces
this by bluntly saying to himself, "To hell with worrying about
where the ball goes, I'm just going to hit it and find it!" He just
lets it happen and accepts the result. In fact, "let it happen"
seems to be the unspoken motto of most of the greatest golfers.

How you reach this level of "trust" will depend somewhat
on your personal philosophies and beliefs. Some players, for
example, have come to believe that "fate" has a hand in outcome. As Jack Nicklaus has said, " . . . there's no doubt that a
certain amount of fatalism regarding the game has contributed heavily to my career by helping me handle the hard
fact that you are always going to lose more than you win."

Others believe a higher power is at work. David Ogrin,
Loren Roberts, and Tom Lehman are examples of devout
Christians who have become more process-oriented by surren-

dering their concerns for outcome to a higher power. For years, Roberts was regarded as one of the better players on Tour who had yet to win a tournament. But he was also regarded as a perfectionist whose levels of emotion after missed shots or putts left him unable to play to his full potential. He knew the problem and began to wonder if he could ever be able to accept his mistakes without allowing his emotions to take over and fill him with negative, self-defeating thoughts. In 1994, he interrupted this cycle by strengthening his spiritual beliefs and adopting the attitude that he must put his energies into managing things within his control, leaving the rest to his higher power. "The real goal is not winning a golf tournament," he said, "but exercising self-control and yielding to God's will—not letting the bad circumstances get me down. . . . Wanting to please God and honor Him with my thoughts and emotions, I was determined to win this inner battle."

After twelve years of trying to win golf tournaments, Loren shifted his mindset to the objective of letting himself win. And he did. His first victory was the Nestle Invitational in 1994. Here he successfully relied on his higher power to help him emotionally as he pressed on with focus and confidence, even after hitting less than perfect shots.

Nick Price, a standout after years of average play, is an example of a player who turned himself around by learning to make every shot of equal importance, leaving results more to luck or circumstance. "I play and give each shot 100 percent," he says. "I'm not thinking about winning or about what score I'm shooting. I'm just doing my best on every shot. If you do that, when you add it up at the end of the day, it should be a pretty good score."

Nick said this while reflecting on the thirty events he played between August 1992 to August 1993, when he won nine times, finished second or third six times, and was in the top ten in twenty-one of the thirty events. For a sustained period of time, Nick became one of the very best at focusing all of his mental energies into playing the shot at hand.

Some Steps for Effective Process-Thinking

Here are several simple steps to help you shift from outcome-thinking to process-thinking. How will you know if they're working? When you feel less pressure, the game gets simpler, and your rounds become a lot more fun.

1. List Outcome Challenges

Before you begin your round, identify all the outcome-oriented thoughts you are likely to battle on that given day. An important key in making this list is to keep in mind the things you truly cannot control: the weather, bad bounces, poor conditions, pairings, tee times, what other players do, and bad luck. These concerns will control you if you let them. They can push you into outcome-thinking, which is related to the not-allowed thoughts we covered in Chapter 2. This includes overconcern with score, position, bets, money, fear of failure, what others think of you when you fail, and the like. All players have these thoughts, but champions are better prepared to recognize them under the pressure of play and replace them with what they can control: the process.

2. Set Process Goals

Before each round, set goals that channel your mental energies into the process. Such goals support your emphasis on the techniques we learned earlier: your sound mental routine and being able to regulate your thoughts. Here are some process goals:

- ○ Be fully committed to your shots and putts before stepping up to the ball. If you are not committed, back off, recommit, and start again.
- ○ Get a definite target for every shot and a definite line for every putt.
- ○ Relax enough to visualize every shot and putt before stepping up to the ball.

○ Feel a smooth tempo for every shot and putt in your practice swing or stroke and in your real swing or stroke.
○ Walk and talk with confidence between shots.
○ Take mental breaks from your round between shots.
○ Stay with your game plan, regardless of your score.

3. Use Emotions as a Cue

Prepare yourself to use your emotions as a cue, or reminder, to adjust from outcome-thinking to process-thinking both before and during competition. These steps will organize your efforts:

○ Try to recognize immediately when emotions are rising—fear, dread, and worry in particular.
○ Recognize that these emotions are a result of nonconstructive outcome-thinking and identify the source.
○ Use these feelings as a friendly reminder to shift your emphasis from the outcome back to the process. Recommit to your mental goals.
○ Judge your process, not your results.

4. Shots and Putts

Refuse to judge your shots and putts by where they stop. Instead, assess your process, such as the quality of your mental routine. If you conclude that any part of the mental routine was weak, challenge yourself to make it better on the next shot.

5. Scores and Positions

Judge your rounds not by your score but by your commitment to your mental goals. After you've played, decide what you could improve physically and incorporate that into your practice. Then decide what you can improve mentally and use that as a goal for your next competitive round.

GOLFPSYCH TECHNIQUE:
Margins for Error

Emotional players—especially perfectionists—who learn to detach from their mistakes usually improve considerably. If you find yourself frequently reacting emotionally to missed shots and putts, we strongly encourage you to learn to create what we call "margins for error."

Perspective: To start, bring yourself closer to reality by considering that the very best player on the PGA Tour:

○ Will miss fairways at least 20 percent of the time;
○ Does not get on the green in regulation at least 25 percent of the time;
○ Will average, at the very best, 1.7 putts per green.

"Guestimate" basic margins: Considering these numbers reflect the best golfers in the world, most of whom are gifted athletes who have competed and worked on their games almost their entire lives, we ask that you "guestimate" reasonable and realistic percentages for yourself. Because it is a guess, this should take only moments. If you are an expert perfectionist, you will likely be tempted to come up with a complex formula to give yourself a defined answer. Resist this temptation as it defeats the purpose of this exercise. Simpler yet, roll your estimations into one percentage number. For example, you might decide that you should accept that at least 25 percent of your total play could be less than your ideal. If you expect that you should hit every fairway, be on every green in regulation, and one-putt every green, your margin is zero. Comparing yourself to the best, your margin should be about 20–25 percent. Now you must adjust for other variables.

Set "adjusted margins": Now you can calculate your adjusted margin for error. Assume the percentage you just gave yourself was on a perfect day, playing a perfect course, with your best game, feeling great, and with no distractions. Before your next competitive round, take into account the following:

- ○ the difficulty of the course and its condition
- ○ your familiarity with the course
- ○ your current peace of mind and health
- ○ the strength of your physical and mental games
- ○ the weather
- ○ possible distractions, expectations, and perceived pressure

Now adjust your percentage higher to account for all of these variables.

Application: You are ready for the very simple, but challenging task of using your margin for error.

As you prepare to compete, anticipate a great round but prepare to accept your predetermined percentage of less-than-desirable shots and putts. Then create an imaginary basket for the undesirable shots and putts. Label it with your percentage. Imagine taking your basket into competition with you. Keep your imaginary basket with you as you play your entire round. Your goal is to mentally "tag" any less-than-desirable shot or putt as part of your margin for error within two seconds after execution. Once tagged, imagine tossing it into your basket. Leave it there until the completion of your round. Don't worry about it. Don't allow it to frustrate or upset you. You knew it could happen. Think about it after the round.

PERSONALIZATION:
Nanci Bowen

After regaining her LPGA Tour card in 1994, Nanci Bowen wanted more than anything to win a tournament, especially a major. When she found herself in contention at the Dinah Shore in Palm Desert, California, in 1995, it took every speck of mental energy Nanci had to detach herself emotionally and stay mentally involved with the process of playing one shot at a time.

She started her last round in the second-to-last group, playing behind three very strong competitors—Nancy Lopez, Laura Davies, and Tammie Green. Her process goals for the day were definite targets, good pictures of her shots, and good tempo, especially with her putts. She vowed not to get involved with her score or that of the others, especially the players ahead of her on the leader board. Another of Nanci's goals was to keep her mind clear and carefree between shots.

Stubbornly refusing to depart from her goals, Nanci successfully committed to her targets, visualized her shots, and used great tempo in her swings and strokes. She managed to avoid looking at the many scoreboards positioned all around the course—until she reached the eighteenth hole.

On seventeen, she'd sunk a difficult, twenty-foot putt and felt a surge of excitement. Then on eighteen, a par five with water surrounding the green, she hit her worst drive of the tournament, blocking the shot into the trees to the right of the fairway. She was walking down the final fairway when she "accidentally slipped a peek" at the closest leader board and felt even more emotion as she realized that the putt on seventeen had given her the lead.

This was a difficult time. She immediately was overwhelmed with outcome thoughts—in no small part because of her incredible desire to win. She began to think of what a win could do for her career. She also began to think what the other players behind her might shoot coming in. Would her lead hold up? Because of these distracting thoughts, her second shot was a six-iron punch that hit the branch of a eucalyptus tree.

Before setting up to the ball again, Nanci knew she had to regroup. She had to get back to her goals by settling herself, committing fully to the shot at hand, and telling herself to forget the outcome of any shot until the completion of play. Her third shot was a smooth three-iron punch short of the water. This left Nanci with a challenging 121-yard approach shot. But after calming herself, she successfully reached the green with a smooth 9-iron. She two putted for bogey.

She'd dropped a stroke to par, but the truth was that after her first two shots, a six was a very good score—and had she not gotten her mind back to process-thinking, her score could easily have been much worse. As it turned out, Nanci finished with a one-stroke lead over her closest competitor—and a lifetime to celebrate winning an LPGA major.

Four

Dominance

○

△

"The biggest mistake amateur players make is hitting a driver into trouble when they can hit a three-wood and stay short of any problems."

Lee Janzen

If a persistent and overwhelming urge to hit the ball as far as you can sometimes—or, worse, always—interferes with strategy, or if a desire to force opportunities displaces patience, you probably are one of those golfers who plays the game with too much "dominance." Being a very aggressive golfer does have one tempting advantage—it can lead to really low scores on days when you are magically lucky. Unfortunately the trade-off is not worth it because more often than not, too much dominance can result in some very high numbers.

On the other hand, there are those who play the game very cautiously, who swing the club tentatively to protect a good start or squander opportunities by refusing to take any risks. This approach has its advantages in that it reduces the odds of making reckless mistakes. But it also significantly reduces scoring opportunities. Such players are too submissive and are unlikely to reach their potential because they never shoot very low scores.

What these two types of players have in common, however, is that they both can approach peak performance by learning to manage their dominance as champions do.

In this chapter we will explore the level of dominance that is best suited to golf. Dominance, as we refer to it here, represents a player's basic competitiveness, assertiveness, and aggressiveness during a round of golf. Our work with champion golfers indicates that the best opportunity for success comes with an above average—but not too high above average—degree of dominance. In comparison, some sports, such as football, hockey, rugby, and boxing, reward high levels of dominance and aggression. Golf definitely does not.

THE CHAMPION GOLFER

The champion golfer strives to maintain a moderately aggressive approach to his play. He is capable of the following:

○ Developing a game plan for managing the course that rewards both patience and assertive play.
○ Implementing a strategy for playing the course that both challenges and maximizes his physical skills.
○ Sticking to the plan regardless of the possibility of shooting a very high or very low score.
○ Striving to maintain the tempo of the swing and stroke that is characteristic of his game.
○ Using normal, full, and confident swings regardless of the score or circumstances.
○ Feeling his score adequately represents his physical abilities most of the time—assuming his mental skills are strong.

To further understand the dominance of a champion, let's review the tendencies of an overly aggressive golfer. This person is assertive, competitive, headstrong, and even stubborn. He experiences his golf in some or all of the following ways:

○ Finds himself better suited to courses that reward aggressive play.
○ Plays more aggressively, to "make up" lost strokes when he faces a high score.
○ Swings harder and faster when faced with the possibility of a low score.
○ Becomes more aggressive and forceful in pressure situations.
○ Swings quickly and aggressively in general and gets even faster under pressure.
○ Sees his scores fluctuate considerably from his good days to his bad.

Now, let's compare these with the tendencies of an overly submissive golfer. This humble person is considerate, conforming, and very easy to get along with in most situations. His characteristics are as follows:

○ Plays his best on courses requiring extreme patience and minimal risk-taking.
○ Wants to protect a low score with guarded, careful play.
○ "Steers" the ball in an effort to minimize the damage when he starts shooting high scores.
○ Feels compelled when under pressure to change his game plan, choosing more conservative shots.
○ Has a smooth and rhythmical swing, except when under pressure.
○ Scores fairly consistently but seldom low enough to be as competitive as his skills would indicate.

You should not be surprised if you experience some tendencies from both lists. Many golfers find that they fluctuate between the two. Often the reason can be put down to ebbs and flows in confidence.

What Are Your Tendencies?

Compare your tendencies to those listed in this simple chart. Keep in mind that 1 represents someone who is extremely submissive; 10 represents someone who is extremely dominant; and 5 to 6 represents someone who is balanced between the two traits. Estimate at which point of the scale you might score on this trait based on *your* personal and golfing tendencies, then circle that number.

Submissive								**Dominant**	
1	**2**	**3**	**4**	**5**	**6**	**7**	**8**	**9**	**10**

PERSONAL TENDENCIES:

Passive	Aggressive
Compliant	Stubborn
Docile	Forceful
Easygoing	Headstrong
Protective	Risk-taker
Tends to follow	Tends to lead

GOLFING TENDENCIES:

Careful	Daring
Waits for opportunities	Forces opportunities
Prefers low-risk shots	Prefers high-risk shots
Consistent mediocre scores	Inconsistent high and low scores

The champions either are or strive to be slightly more dominant, or aggressive, in the way they play, including managing the course and swinging the club. They resist forcing opportunities and they avoid careful, passive play.

Players Who Are More Submissive

Al Geiberger, Ed Dougherty, and Jackie Gallagher-Smith are all examples of great players who are naturally more submissive and easygoing, yet who have learned to use planned assertiveness to reach many competitive goals.

Players Who Are More Dominant

Dave Stockton, Lanny Wadkins, Dottie Pepper, and Brett Ogle are examples of players who test to be very competitive and aggressive, yet who have learned to direct their forcefulness toward the goal of playing with great strategy and finesse instead of simple force.

We do not suggest that players who naturally have a perfect level of dominance for golf are not victim to some of the above tendencies. In fact, they sometimes lose their competitiveness because of weaknesses in several of the other champion traits. Some of the other challenges to maintaining competitive dominance include emotional stability, confidence, and tension. Let's take them one by one.

Emotional stability: Al D'Amato (no relation to the former U.S. Senator) is an excellent amateur player who turned fifty several years ago. He lives in Southern California, has a successful forklift business, and has competed in numerous amateur events over the years, many with only moderate success.

It was with the best of intentions that, in 1994, fellow Southern California golfer and former USC teammate of Al Geiberger, Bob Foote gave Al D'Amato a copy of a GolfPsych newsletter titled "Emotional Stability." As he read the newsletter, Al realized that the emotional outbursts that followed errant shots were sabotaging him.

Al took our personality questionnaire, received his Golf-Psych Report and began working on taming his emotional outbursts. As a result of learning to manage his emotions, Al found it easier to use one of the important strengths revealed

by his profile—a great measure of dominance and competitiveness.

In his old pattern, Al became less emotionally stable and
more dominant as his rounds progressed. He would become
more aggressive trying to make up shots and that only increased the intensity of his emotions. By the time he'd have
completed his round, Al would have abandoned his game
plan, quickened his swing, and lost his ability to make smart
decisions.

We explained to Al how his emotions were hampering his
competitive dominance. He came to understand that habits of
thought influenced his emotions, whereupon his emotions led
to increased aggression, a faster swing, high-risk decisions, and
poor play.

His efforts to change produced results that were both
immediate and dramatic. Within months of beginning the
process, Al was playing with finesse instead of force. In 1995,
he qualified for the U.S. Senior Open.

Driven by this early success, Al continued to work on his
emotions. In 1997, at fifty-seven, he qualified for the U.S. Amateur, a tournament crowded with college players. He was the
oldest player in the field by far.

Confidence: When confidence goes, even the most aggressive players will find themselves holding onto their shots,
steering clubs, and guiding strokes. When you lose confidence
in part of your game, you tend to respond based on your natural level of dominance. For example, if your putting is off
and you are more dominant, you probably will work harder to
get on the greens in regulation and closer to the hole. This
can lead to shooting at "sucker" pins and trying to hit impossible shots. If you are more submissive, you probably will
emphasize lagging every putt near the hole to avoid three-
putting.

Tension: High tension seems to take submissiveness and
dominance to their respective extremes. Whatever is most natural for you is exaggerated with tension. For those with dominance ratings above the champion levels, tension will cause

them to be more aggressive with every shot or putt, trying to play shots the best players in the world might not even try. Those with low dominance ratings, the submissive player, will go into careful and deliberate mode, making choices that are sometimes ridiculously safe.

ARE YOU TOO DOMINANT OR NOT DOMINANT ENOUGH?

Complete this self-evaluation by applying the numerical values below to your answers.

1: Always   2: Often   3: Sometimes   4: Seldom   5: Never

___ A. I get protective or "steery" with my swing or stroke when uncomfortable.

___ B. I choose high-risk shots that offer me less than a 50 percent chance of success.

___ C. I will change my strategy for playing the course to make up strokes or protect a good score.

___ D. My swing or strokes get forceful and aggressive when I feel pressure.

___ E. I prefer to manage the course with a strategy that requires I take no more risks than are absolutely necessary.

_____ Total x 2 ÷ 5 = _____ Dominance Rating

If you rated yourself 8 or higher, you probably have the competitiveness and the moderately aggressive approach to play that allows you to maximize your golfing skills. If you scored less than 8, and your scores were low on A and C, you are likely too submissive in your approach to competitive golf. If you scored less than 8, and your scores were low on B and D, you are likely too aggressive in your approach to competitive golf.

If the result of this test suggests that you should work on your dominance, you should start by changing your mental approach in two key areas. The first involves an overall approach to the way you play the game, specifically the way you manage the course. The other involves the degree to which you fully and confidently swing the club to play each individual shot. Either can be too tentative or too aggressive. The former requires better managing and planning skills, the latter requires a change of priorities and objectives. Let's begin with the way you currently manage a golf course.

GOLFPSYCH TECHNIQUE:
Course Management

"The biggest difference between amateurs and pros is course management . . . good course management doesn't always mean playing it safe; it can mean playing aggressively."

Lee Janzen

We believe that, no matter what your handicap, you will have a better game plan for managing the courses you play if you maximize your competitive dominance. The game plan is *your* game with a champion level of dominance.

As soon as a golfer we deal with has the skills to play a full round of golf and is truly interested in getting the lowest score possible, we encourage him to begin developing his game plans. Often we are surprised by the lack of time even some advanced players designate to this part of their game.

Learning or reminding yourself of some of the basics of good course management can get you started:

○ Knowledge of how far you hit the ball with each club when good contact is made.
○ The ability to use scorecards and yardage markers to determine distances to targets, as well as to the front, middle, and backs of greens.
○ An awareness of the speed and firmness of greens.

○ The ability and discipline to choose targets, clubs, and types of shots for the course you are playing that are based on your skills and not on emotions, impulse, what you think is expected by others, ego, or an over-concern with results.

As your skills evolve, so should your basic tools for course management. They might include:

○ Developing confidence in the clubs you will need for the course you are playing.
○ Knowing the different characteristics of the various grasses on golf courses, such as bent, Bermuda, Kikuyu, and so on.
○ Planning for possible conditions, such as wind, moisture, and temperature changes.
○ Estimating likely pin placements.
○ Deciding on a strategy that maximizes the use of your evolving skills while still ensuring a better than fifty-fifty chance of successfully executing the shots you have chosen.

If you do not currently have a strategy for developing your game plan, you might want to make this at least one of your lessons with a qualified teaching professional. Here's a simple, yet effective approach should you choose to go it alone.

Write down the clubs and types of shots you currently feel are your strongest. Estimate yardages for each. Gather any printed information you may have on the course, ideally a map or a scorecard that shows the layout and the length of the holes. Include pin sheets and yardage books when they are available. With this information in hand, follow the steps that were outlined in Chapter 1 under the heading GolfPsych Technique: The Three-Step Mental Preshot Routine (page 42) and in Chapter 2 under the heading GolfPsych Technique:

Basic Preparation for Both Concrete and Abstract Thinkers (page 64).

Once you have a real plan for playing the course that is moderately aggressive and based on your skills, strive to remain as committed to that plan as possible. Change your plan only when weather and conditions require it.

Most good players solidify their game plan for competition during their practice rounds. Because this may require some trial and error, you may find it more productive to forget about scoring or betting during such a round. Confirm your plan for playing every hole with the probable conditions. Establish a firm commitment to your clubs, targets, and the types of shots for each hole, paying special attention to the difficult ones. And remember—your goal is to make choices that match your skills and maximize your opportunities on each hole.

Champions are very aware of their personal tendencies in specific situations and develop their game plans accordingly. You should do likewise.

If you are a dominant and aggressive person, you should resist choosing any shot that you could not successfully execute at least six out of ten times on the practice tee. Also, because the dominant player tends to have a fast, aggressive swing, when between clubs you should choose less club and just swing normally. By doing this, you're avoiding the situation in which you feel you have too much club—a situation where dominant players swing more guardedly and unnaturally. But most important, resist trying to aggressively make up for lost strokes by changing your game plan or by swinging harder and faster.

If you are a submissive player, choose one or two holes a round that you will play a bit more aggressively, but still within your control. When between clubs, take more club and maintain a smooth, rhythmic swing. When your score is low, don't get careful and protective; stay committed to your game plan, your swing, and your mental routine.

GOLFPSYCH TECHNIQUE:
Competitive Priorities and Objectives

Every GolfPsych Technique is aimed at developing your best competitive priorities. To stay competitive, it is vital that you commit to the following before each round:

○ Give the process of your play a greater priority than the outcome of your play. In other words, remain committed to your routine, tempo, and game plan rather than let yourself get overly involved with the results of shots, score, and position. This will allow you the peace of mind to remain effectively competitive. In addition, having great tempo on every shot and putt is the key to making natural, full, uninhibited, and unforced swings. This will prevent you from getting protective, careful, guided, or forceful in the way you swing the club.

○ Regulate your thoughts between shots. These mental breaks help keep you from getting overly aggressive or tentative in an effort to make the best use of your skills.

PERSONALIZATION:
Ed Dougherty

Ed Dougherty is known among his peers for being kind and easygoing. He's also known for his hard work, perseverance, determination, and stamina. Having played the PGA Tour for twenty-four years, he has been accurately described as a journeyman pro. " 'Grinding' is Ed's middle name," says Tour rules official and former pro Slugger White.

Ed first joined the tour in 1975 and that same year he played with Jack Nicklaus in the final group of the PGA Championship at Firestone. Ed got stuck in a bunker and shot 77.

Nicklaus won. Because of that, Ed usually felt that he was competing against players with far more natural abilities, who did not seem to have to work quite as hard on their games, and who maybe approached the game a little more aggressively than he did.

Ed's philosophy had long been, "play for pars and let birdies happen." In many ways that philosophy had paid off for him. Ed often played his way into the final group, but until July 1995 he had never won.

At the time of the Deposit Guaranty Classic in Madison, Mississippi, Ed was forty-seven years old and had been sidelined with a torn chest muscle for almost six months. He had lost his PGA Tour exempt status and had played in only two other events that year. All in all, Ed had every reason to revert to submissive or emotional decision making during this tournament. But, persistent as ever, he did not. In fact, he began playing more aggressively, perhaps with a bit more of the attitude that there was much to gain and little to lose.

Ed shot a first round 68, followed it with another 68, and then a third-round 70 that left him three strokes behind Dicky Thompson and among fifteen players within four shots of the lead. Late in his fourth round, when he crossed the bridge that leads to the eighteenth green at Annandale Golf Club, Ed held a two-stroke lead.

The eighteenth hole is a 532-yard par five, with water down the left side of the fairway and in front of the green. Ed knew he had a two-stroke lead and that Gil Morgan—who was with him in the final group—was chasing him. (Thompson, also in the group, had already faltered on the back nine.) Ed had to make a rational decision. Not only was he poised to win his first PGA Tour event after twenty years of blood, sweat, and tears, but he also had a shot to earn an invitation to the Masters and to secure his playing privileges for the next two years. He'd then be fifty and eligible for the Senior PGA Tour.

It was tempting to protect his score and position by playing the hole as conservatively as possible and guiding his swing to try to prevent error, but Ed was determined that he would not give in to excitement, fear, excessive desire, or an urge to protect or to force an opportunity. Ed calmly assessed his odds, his confidence, and his composure before deciding how to best play the hole. In line with his game plan, and supported by his composure and confidence, he decided on and committed to his driver, the left side of the fairway, and a fade.

Feeling great about his odds, Ed totally forgot about outcome and hit the ball just as he had imagined, leaving himself 239 yards to the hole. His choices were to lay up to within an easy wedge, or to hit a 220-yard carry into the green.

His usual choice would have been the more conservative one, but at this moment Ed knew he was both relaxed and confident enough to use his 5-wood. Ed felt the odds were with him as he chose to fade the shot well over the water and onto the green. Again he hit the shot he had imagined. He then two-putted from 60 feet and won his first PGA Tour event.

Ed simply had worked out a great plan for his game and had stuck with it. He managed his submissiveness and won.

Five

Tough-Mindedness

○

△

"Give me the wind, bad weather, bumpy greens, and slow play—it all gives me an advantage because I know I'm mentally prepared to handle it while a lot of other players aren't."

Dave Stockton

The oft-heard quote by crusty baseball manager Leo Durocher that "nice guys finish last" doesn't always apply in golf. Either the nice guys that play golf have learned to be more tough-minded in competition or the tough-minded competitors (whom Durocher probably thought finished first) have learned to display most of their selfish and unlikable behavior when away from the course. Tough-mindedness is a trait that does come more naturally to the not-so-nice guys, but with a little determination, all serious golfers, even the nicest, can become a little tougher.

Tough-mindedness, as we refer to it here, involves several things, including:

1. The skill or ability to accept and prepare for challenges over which you have little or no control, such as gamesmanship, poor conditions, or slow play.
2. The skill or ability to detach emotionally from outside variables, such as the bad play of a close friend and playing partner or a desire to please others with the quality of your play or even unrelated problems tied to business, family, or friends.
3. The skill or ability to remain somewhat selfish in your approach to competition, placing priority on your own needs and concerns while competing.

Dave Stockton is a great example of the nice guy who finds it more natural to be likable than tough-minded. Early in his Senior Tour career, Dave showed mental strength in the first two of the three areas listed above, but we found a definite need to strengthen his tough-mindedness with regard to the third. In other words, he needed to be more selfish.

As I worked a Senior Tour event early one season, it intrigued me to hear in each of my first five sessions how each player had recently received a putting lesson from Dave. When does he work on his own game? I wondered.

Knowing of his success and popularity in conducting corporate outings, it's not surprising that Dave enjoys sharing his knowledge with others—especially when he is asked to help. When I saw Dave later that day, I had to smile when one of the comments he made to me was "My putting is off—I haven't had much time to work on it." After some friendly ribbing, we discussed his helping others at the expense of his own game. Of course it's great for him to help others, just as long as he worked on his own game first. Dave didn't need much convincing and agreed to make being a nice guy secondary to thinking like a champion.

THE CHAMPION GOLFER

Champion golfers have a remarkable ability to enter competition using above average tough-mindedness and detaching themselves emotionally from the many adversities that can diminish their focus. They retain this mental approach in spite of the distractions they might bring to the course and the distractions they encounter on the course.

Off the golf course they have the equally remarkable ability to be more tender and caring with family and friends, giving themselves the stability needed to endure the "ups and downs" of life itself.

One of the distinguishing aspects of champions is their understanding of how much being tough-minded can influence their play. They also understand what they must do to stay tough-minded. As with all aspects of the mental game, the first step to becoming tough-minded is to become aware of tendencies.

When we test for the tough-minded vs. tender-minded tendencies of our clients, we measure with a one-to-ten scale using one for tough-minded and ten for tender-minded. Champions are in the three-to-four range, having above-average tendencies toward being tough-minded when they compete. Those who test to be very tender-minded, almost without exception, find their games improve as they take a more tough-minded approach toward competition. Those who test to be very tough-minded often find that the quality of their relationships and personal lives improve as they take a more tender-minded approach to relating with friends and loved ones. To their surprise, this often enhances their golf as well.

What Are Your Tendencies?

Compare your tendencies to those listed in this simple chart. Keep in mind that 1 represents someone who is extremely tough-minded; 10 represents someone who is extremely tender-minded; and 5 to 6 represents someone who is a combination of the two traits, or who is balanced between the two. Estimate at which point of the scale you might score on this trait based on *your* personal and golfing tendencies, then circle that number.

Tough-Minded							Tender-Minded		
1	**2**	**3**	**4**	**5**	**6**	**7**	**8**	**9**	**10**

PERSONAL TENDENCIES:

Selfish	Caring
Indifferent	Sensitive
Practical	Intuitive
Emotionally detached	Emotionally involved
Easily says "no"	Has difficulty saying "no"

GOLFING TENDENCIES:

Helps self first	Helps others first
Challenged by bad conditions	Distracted by bad conditions
Detached from gamesmanship	Affected by gamesmanship
Indifferent to others	Concerned for others

The champions either are or strive to be considerably more tough-minded in competition. They can selfishly channel their efforts and thoughts into themselves and their play to maximize effectiveness and minimize distractions.

Players Who Are More Tough-Minded

Champion golfers who find that tough-mindedness comes a bit more naturally to them are Greg Norman and Craig Stadler. They can direct personal concerns toward themselves and their golf when they compete, and detach themselves from all issues detrimental to their play. Yet, even these players must at times take extra steps to keep their tough-mindedness for competition.

Such was the case with Greg Norman when he found

himself immersed in a multitude of other business ventures. He had to take steps to fully delegate many of the responsibilities so that he could comfortably, completely, and selfishly direct his full attention to his golf while competing. Even the tough-minded champion Craig Stadler finds it more challenging to selfishly focus on his own career while his two sons, Kevin and Chris, excel in their respective sports of golf and football, and his wife, Sue, operates her own successful decorating business.

Players Who Are More Tender-Minded

Dave Stockton, Al Geiberger, Doug Martin, Katie Peterson, and Jackie Gallagher-Smith are more sensitive, caring, and concerned for others to the point of almost letting their approach to life interfere with their play. Al Geiberger is a gentle soul who can find it hard to selfishly manage his time because of the difficulty he finds in saying "no" to others. Dave Stockton, who is more assertive but still tender-minded, has on numerous occasions taken time between shots to ask Senior Tour on-course officials for an update on his son's play at a concurrent PGA Tour event. Doug Martin, who's played the PGA Tour since 1992, is a devoted father and husband who finds it difficult to leave his wife, Gaylyn, and their two children to go on the road, especially when he is not playing his best. He has learned to deal with this more effectively. Doug challenges himself to have a more tough-minded attitude when dealing with difficult circumstances to get the most out of his time on Tour. As a result, he gets the absolute most out of his game, which in turn affords him more quality time with his family.

The dual and opposing requirements of being tough-minded for competition and tender-minded in relationships can make achieving this trait confusing and difficult for those who score at either extreme of this scale. Players with extreme tendencies, such as the tough-minded player who is emotionally-detached from his family or the tender-minded player who is extremely sensitive to the opinions of others, benefit most from personal counseling with a qualified, licensed therapist.

THE TOUGH-MINDED GOLFER

If you are a tough-minded individual, you will likely find yourself more naturally a tough-minded golfer. If so, you will more readily say "no" to someone with whom you do not want to play or to someone who wants to interrupt your practice or schedule with their own needs or agenda. You will also find it much easier to temporarily detach yourself from your personal and family problems while playing golf, thereby allowing you to conserve your mental energy for the game. In addition, you will find it much easier to detach yourself from gamesmanship or the painfully poor play of a likable playing partner. Such characteristics can enhance your competitiveness in that they make it less likely you will play with a busy or troubled mind.

As we mentioned, these same characteristics can have a detrimental affect on your personal life, making it difficult to establish or maintain healthy relationships with significant others. This can lead to less stable marriages, strained relationships with children, or difficulties keeping true friends. While you may not see or feel daily effects on your performance, over the long haul, you will likely experience periodic ups and downs in your play when personal problems occur. Rather than use golf as an escape from these common problems, you will help yourself and those you care about (and your golf) by making solving them the top priority.

While the tender-minded characteristics are not well-suited to playing golf successfully, they can help you attain the peace of mind necessary to play your best. It appears that champion golfers with the greatest longevity and fewest "lows" in their careers are also the players who have dedicated time toward maintaining quality relationships with their wives and families.

Some great examples are Jack Nicklaus, Gary Player, Raymond Floyd, and Dave Stockton. Nicklaus credits his family as one of the major reasons for his longevity. Player may be the most traveled athlete in the history of golf with his many trips from the PGA and Senior Tours to be with his family in his native South Africa. Floyd has maintained a very supportive team with his wife, Maria, and his three children. Dave Stockton has lived with his best friend and greatest fan—his wife, Cathy—for almost three decades. She is endlessly supportive of Dave and his goals, which is easy to do because of Dave's sensitivity, concern, and care for her. He even good-naturedly accepts reminders when he forgets to set aside enough quality time for her and her concerns. To this day she accompanies him enthusiastically to every event possible.

Did you notice a common thread? Each of these players will credit a strong marital partnership as having contributed immeasurably to their enduring success. While it is not a prerequisite for success, being tender-minded with significant others contributes immensely to the peace of mind needed for peak performance.

A TOUGH-MINDED TEST

Answer the following questions, applying the point values listed below.

1: Always   2: Often   3: Sometimes   4: Seldom   5: Never

___ A. When I feel extremely frustrated while playing, I give up and stop trying.

___ B. I find myself distracted by the mannerisms, habits, attitudes, or play of my playing partners.

___ C. I find myself giving up time for my preshot routine to help others find their lost balls.

___ D. I have a hard time saying "no" to someone asking for help with their game, even though it takes away what little time I have to work on my own.

___ E. When I play, I find myself worrying about the opinions, thoughts, and concerns of other people.

___ F. Bad weather, poor conditions, or slow play can really negatively affect my play.

_____ Total x 2 ÷ 6 = _____ Tough-Minded Rating

If you rated yourself eight or higher, you likely are very tough-minded in competition. Be sure you are more tender-minded with friends and loved ones. If you rated lower than eight, you will need to decide if playing better golf is worth being more tough-minded on the course, especially in competition. If you do decide it is, familiarize yourself with the thoughts and attitudes of the champions and use this chapter to increase your tough-mindedness.

IS IT WORTH IT?

Before taking steps to be more tough-minded, you must decide on your true priority for playing the game. Which is more important to you—to be a great social golfer, using the sport as a medium to meet, entertain, teach, or get to know people? Or to be a great competitor, getting the most from the natural and trained skills you have developed? If you play golf for purely social reasons, you probably need not concern yourself with developing tough-mindedness. But if you want to be a great competitor, you will want to be as tough-minded as possible while playing.

This is not to say that you must be cold and indifferent to be successful. You must discipline yourself to remain emotionally uninvolved with what others are thinking, feeling, and doing while you are competing. You must keep your thoughts simple, emotions even, focus narrow, and your mind at peace while hitting each of your shots and putts.

You can, for example, say "nice shot" without getting emotionally involved with how another player is feeling or how much they are enjoying their day. Or you can choose to experience little or no concern about how another player views your game, regardless of who they are or what they themselves have accomplished. It is possible to do both and remain mindful enough of playing partners to compete with etiquette. You can even help a fellow golfer with his game, just not before or during a competitive round if it will in any way interfere with your own game and preparation.

Having made the choice to be tough-minded, keep in mind that there are still circumstances that can interfere, even if you come by the trait naturally. These include having to change from tender to tough quickly, often due to hectic business schedules, personal issues, and fatigue.

Take the case of club and teaching professionals. They face a particularly tough challenge in that their jobs frequently require dual and opposing roles with regards to this and a few of the other champion traits. On one hand, their positions require that they be very tender-minded in that they must have a genuine interest in and concern for the happiness, enjoyment, and success of others in order to be truly good at their jobs. At the same time they often are expected to be competitive, demonstrating the skills they teach by effectively representing their clubs in tournaments. Never mind that they get little time to practice and that, when they do, they are still expected to be mindful of club and member needs.

The golf professional in this position represents the extreme example of a golfer who must learn to change hats quickly and effectively. With practice, even the busy teacher can learn to switch from the very tender-minded teacher to the moderately tender-minded manager to the tough-minded competitor.

The equivalent in the amateur ranks would be the golfer who rushes from the office to the course, sometimes with only moments between parking his car and being called to the first tee. Without realizing it, he takes the concerns of the day onto the course. If you find yourself with ten minutes or less of warm-up, the best use of your time will not involve hitting shots but relaxing, clearing your mind and giving yourself a simple mental goal for the day.

A few of the most tough-minded players seem to concentrate better the more chaotic their lives become. Such players may be knowingly or unwittingly using the game as a mental break or temporary escape from their present worries. But this tends to be a short-term phenomenon. Resistance and the ability to block out these worries typically breaks down, play deteriorates, and the problems must be resolved before these golfers can resume good play.

Whether you are naturally more tender-minded or you are made more so by circumstances such as those just described, the techniques provided here can be very effective in helping you strengthen your skills and abilities. These techniques are among our most popular and have proven to be effective, fun, and easy for players of all ages, levels, and abilities.

GOLFPSYCH TECHNIQUE:
Create an Attitude for Competition

The attitude you take into competition has a great deal to do with your ability to maintain a dominant and competitive approach to your play. Before your round, take a few moments to check your attitude. If you find yourself feeling fear, dread, low confidence, or other inhibitors, use relaxation and imagery to create the attitude you want for competition.

Identifying thoughts and feelings during your best play can be invaluable to you for creating your desired attitude for competition. Follow these steps:

1. Draw or trace a circle or oval in the middle of a large, blank page so that the circle or oval takes up one-half to two-thirds of the available space.

2. Now take a few moments to fully relax, closing your eyes if necessary, and reflect on your last best competitive tournament, round, or several holes of golf. Try to imagine as vividly as possible what you were thinking and feeling, how you were walking and talking, and the circumstances surrounding your good play.

3. Once you have your image, write inside your circle the positive and specific words or phrases that describe your thoughts and feelings before and during your play that day. Write as many items as possible, whether trite, redundant, or strange. If you have trouble remembering or describing how you felt, read through this sample list of items we most frequently hear from golfers of all levels and use those to which you can relate.

Calm
Peaceful Relaxed
Confident Focused Patient
In-the-moment Happy
Resilient   Committed to clubs
Committed to types of shots
Good rhythm Good tempo
Good targets First impressions
Great touch Great feel Carefree
Easy Fun Decisive Simple
Definite game plan

4. After completing your list, take a few moments to practice creating your attitude for competition, just as you would do prior to the first tee shot of your next round. Get in as relaxed a state as possible. Lie or sit in a com-

fortable position with your neck relaxed, arms and legs uncrossed. Using progressive relaxation—deep breathing or another favored form of relaxing—release all tension from your body.

5. Once fully relaxed, vividly imagine yourself feeling all the things listed inside your circle. For example, with the word "confident," try to see yourself walking and talking with confidence; hear yourself giving yourself compliments; feel the pride and comfort that comes with believing in yourself and trusting your skills.

6. Now imagine yourself driving to the course, warming-up, practicing, and playing the first hole with these same feelings and thoughts.

GOLFPSYCH TECHNIQUE:
The Imaginary Bubble

A second GolfPsych technique we use is called "the imaginary bubble." It is designed to stop intrusive thoughts or excessive worries that make it difficult to keep your competitive attitude.

Imagery can be a very powerful tool not only for helping you create a competitive attitude but also for keeping it, regardless of the challenges. Using an imaginary bubble not only will help increase your awareness of current distractions and faulty thinking, but it also will help you manage them rather than letting them manage you.

Let's start by identifying all the thoughts, feelings, and circumstances that are likely to interfere with your desired attitude. Think about your last most discouraging round and try to identify the thoughts and feelings that you think interfered with your ability to play your best. Go back to your notes for creating a positive attitude and retrieve your circle. Using the space on the *outside* of your circle, write down the thoughts, problems, or circumstances that interfered with your play.

As you write, consider things outside your control, such as rain delays, slow play, pairings, tee times, and so forth. Also include bad habits of thought, such as self-criticism, self-doubt, fearing the worst, thinking about the opinions of others, analyzing mechanics, and the like. These distractions can also come in the forms of feeling excessive responsibility for helping someone else enjoy their round; wanting to impress someone with your game or your personality; feeling inadequate and self-conscious in the presence of another player or players; or taking responsibility for the slow play or bad manners of another.

Compare your notes to these more specific examples, shown below, of common distractions to thinking like a champion. Those you can relate to should go outside your bubble.

Now take a few moments to practice using your imaginary bubble. Follow the earlier steps for creating your attitude with regards to relaxing your body and imagining the positive attitude that is reflected inside your circle. Once you have created your attitude, imagine pulling around you a safe, clear, protective bubble. Your bubble is to help you contain your champion attitude and repel the items outside your circle that can pull you into being average. Imagine yourself going to the course, practicing, and playing a hole or two with your bubble in place.

Test your ability by reviewing your list of possible distractions then mentally pushing the distractions away from your bubble. They will try to get in. You must imagine keeping them out. Reflecting on a recent frustrating hole or round can illustrate this. First imagine playing the hole as you did, being mindful of everything that could pull you out of your bubble. Now play the hole as you would prefer, this time using your bubble to help deflect the faulty thinking. This imagery practice will prepare you to use your bubble in your next round. It will provide you a strong, positive, confident, and peaceful space in which you will execute your shots and putts. Before beginning your competitive round, challenge yourself to hit as many shots as possible from inside your circle.

We have a few old *Star Trek* fans that find it more fun to use an imaginary "force field" instead of a bubble. Others relate to simply putting themselves in their "golf circle." The objective is the same: To hit as many shots as possible while thinking like a champion. That means refusing to give in to the factors that so readily interfere. Most find it helpful to rewrite their notes on a smaller paper or index card to put in their pocket, bag, or yardage book for easy reference when they play.

PERSONALIZATION:
Caryn Rohrbaugh

Ted Sheftic is a talented and driven PGA of America professional who along with his wife, Tommie, has coordinated golf services for Hanover Country Club in Hanover, Pennsylvania, for many years. Ted's students have included countless club members, nationally ranked amateurs, and LPGA professionals.

Part of his tireless and comprehensive effort toward help-ing his students be the best they can has included his own training as a GolfPsych instructor. He encourages players of all levels to work on their mental skills, ensuring they get maxi-mum benefit from their physical lessons. Caryn Rohrbaugh is one of Ted's students.

Ted referred Caryn for a GolfPsych report because of the difficulty she was having taking her game from the practice area into competition. At the time she was forty-two, married, the mother of two, and a very avid golfer with a seventeen handicap. Caryn had already learned from Ted that she was much too conscious of her swing when she played and was much too aware of what others thought of her. This left her with poor concentration, too much emotion, high tension, and high scores.

After taking the one-hour personality questionnaire, we could see from Caryn's scores that her ability to concentrate was naturally good and very well suited to golf, as was her natural level of tension. Her abilities to manage emotions, make decisions, and effectively think her way around the course were also very strong. Compared to the champion golfer's statistical profile, she scored at or near champion level on six of the eight traits. The other traits that she didn't score as well in were confidence, which was average, and tough-mindedness, which registered the weakest of all. Clearly, her lack of tough-mindedness was affecting her other mental and physical skills.

Through our sessions with Caryn, we learned that she'd been very successful in every other aspect of her life but found golf perplexing and frustrating. Her performance has not matched her efforts to improve. This frustration was hurting her performances, and her handicap was going in the wrong direction.

As is typical with most golfers, Caryn was using only one medium to try to improve: more physical practice and more lessons from Ted. She believed improving her swing mechan-ics would solve her performance problems. Fortunately for

Caryn, Ted recognized that the problems with her performance were not simply swing-based.

Because of Caryn's tender-mindedness she was sensitive to the concerns of others and to how they perceived her. These concerns led to a reduced ability to focus, a busier mind, and greatly reduced mental skills. Often she was more mentally involved with the thoughts and perceptions of others than with the process of playing her own shot. The ensuing poor shots led Caryn to question her fundamentals, to play more mechanically, and, ultimately, to try to fix a mental problem with a physical lesson. Lots of golfers do this.

We began by explaining the connection between her thoughts and her poor performance. We gave her techniques and suggestions for controlling her thoughts before and during play. Imagery was very helpful, as Caryn learned to manage her thoughts regarding others and to minimize her reaction to poor shots and putts. One of the techniques she found most effective was to put her faulty thoughts or bad shots in an imaginary "bad-shot jar." Taking an unusual and extra step to strengthen her imagery, Caryn chose to draw this jar the night before her competitive rounds. Using her kids' brightly colored construction paper and markers to create a paper jar became her symbol and reminder to mentally put away the self-conscious thoughts and errant shots as quickly as possible and to forego concerns about mechanics while playing.

Mental lessons for Caryn over the next several months included steps to build a strong mental game and to "uncondition" some of her bad habits of thought. These steps included setting up a strong mental routine, regulating her thoughts, and focusing on techniques for strengthening her confidence. But the key GolfPsych Technique for bringing all of Caryn's efforts together was to increase tough-mindedness.

Before competing, Caryn took the time to draw a large circle and complete the described steps for creating a positive attitude by using an imaginary bubble. We then instructed Caryn to be sure to complete the next step, writing on the outside of her circle anything she thought might bother her, such as rude playing partners, bumpy greens, memories of past failures, and such.

The night before competition Caryn was to put herself in a relaxed state and imagine playing using her protective bubble and her bad-shot jar. Whenever she noticed thoughts from outside her circle trying to get in, she would imagine pushing them out of her circle.

Caryn soon found herself more tough-minded in competition. She was much better prepared to handle difficult playing partners by remaining undistracted by their antics, rude comments, or play. In addition, her concern about her fundamentals diminished as her mental routine improved.

Caryn's work on her mental game was rewarded with some great play. In that first year, she won her flight in the district tournament; won her club match-play championship—on the twelfth hole!—and lowered her handicap by five or six strokes. The next year she repeated as club champion. Best of all, she is now enjoying competitive golf more than ever.

GOLFPSYCH TECHNIQUE:
Using Adversity as a Cue

Mike Hulbert, John Schroeder, and Dan Forsman are fine examples of other players who have worked successfully toward being more tough-minded in competition, each addressing different tender-minded tendencies in the process. One of the techniques they have incorporated is learning to use adversity as a cue to relax and improve their focus on the shot at hand. This simple technique is very effective for turning frustrations into tools.

Here are some examples of adverse experiences that can be overcome:

○ Fearing bad shots and putts.
○ Remaining self-conscious after hitting bad shots or putts.

○ Feeling hurt, sensitive, or angry after bearing the brunt of a negative comment or action of another.

○ Being hyperaware of your swing and game when shooting an especially low or high score.

In each of these situations, you can turn the bad experience around to strengthen rather than weaken your mental game. Follow these simple steps:

1. Identify "distracting experiences": List all the experiences that are most likely to detract from your tough-minded play, such as mental mistakes, physical mistakes, low scores, large galleries, gamesmanship, noise, perceived or real judgment of others, controversial comments.

2. Choose an "anchor": These are *key words or phrases* that will remind you to return to the clear focus you experience when hitting your best shots. Examples include smooth tempo, definite target, clear visualization of a shot or putt.

3. Convert "detractors" to "cues": Put yourself in a very relaxed state and imagine yourself in a past situation where a detracting experience interfered with your tough-mindedness and focus. Now use your imagery to practice using this detractor as a cue to relax and use your anchor. Mentally replay your shot with the strong image of using your anchor. Each time you have one of your detracting experiences in competition, use it to cue your anchor.

PERSONALIZATION:
Lee Janzen

You will recall how, in chapter two, we discussed how Lee Janzen came into the PGA Championship at Riviera without enough Ryder Cup points to automatically be selected to the team. He would have to win the PGA Championship or be captain's pick to get on the team. The press was well aware of this and, looking for a story, constantly asked Lee the same questions in the weeks leading to the PGA. Lee found this bothersome and distracting, causing him to focus excessively on the outcome. So he chose to use these questions as cues to think about his circle and how well he would use his mental routine to focus on each shot. He prepared for the questions with canned answers so he could stay uninvolved with the questions.

You may also recall that Lee did not win the PGA, was not an automatic selection to the team, and wasn't even a captain's pick. The media's questions intensified, but Lee chose to use this controversy as an even stronger cue to focus on his anchors of "targets" and "tempo" and his mental game the following week at The International. This remained his goal for every hole and for every day. Lee was successful into Sunday's round, where he finished with a flurry of birdies. Lee used the controversy to his advantage and gave the best possible response to not being chosen for the Ryder Cup team: *Winning.*

Six

Confidence

○

△

"Confidence has to be the golfer's greatest single weapon . . .
if he believes he can get the ball into the hole, a lot of the time
he will, even if his technique appears downright faulty."

Jack Nicklaus

Some of the most charmed lives—and golf games—belong to
those who are blessed with great confidence. It is a key to success in everything we do. The way we carry ourselves, communicate, experience relationships, work, relax, and play golf are
all very much influenced by the way we think and feel about
ourselves.

Confidence comes easily to some yet remains a lifelong
pursuit for others. It is one of the more challenging traits to
strengthen, but it can be done. And it certainly is worth the
effort.

We encourage the awareness and development of two
types of confidence: personal confidence and performance
confidence. You will find it helpful to understand the difference between the two and the importance of each.

PERSONAL CONFIDENCE

Personal confidence is considered to be in large part learned and at least some part inherited. It is a measure of your basic self worth, how happy you are with yourself as a person. The truly confident person loves himself, believes in himself, and can give himself compliments along with criticism. He is not so vulnerable to the daily ups-and-downs that can leave the not-so-confident feeling empty, worthless, or incompetent.

It is believed that much of personal confidence is learned through life experiences, especially those of our early years. Parents may unintentionally teach us to think of ourselves in ways that undermine confidence by the approach they use to instruct and discipline us. For example, if a parent frequently reprimands a child by saying, "You are so lazy; can't you do better than that?" the child is likely to think of himself in a negative fashion as he matures. On the other hand, if a parent makes a comparable statement using a more positive slant, such as, "You're a great athlete; keep trying and you will do better!" he will have a more positive influence on a child's personal confidence.

Many other things encountered during someone's lifetime can have a considerable effect on personal confidence. Peers, friendships, relationships, one's birth order, teachers, coaches, illnesses, injuries, learning disabilities, physical disabilities, and varied emotional experiences all contribute to a person's confidence or lack thereof.

PERFORMANCE CONFIDENCE

Performance confidence relates more to learned skills and involves a strong belief in your abilities to play golf at a high level. On the rare day when you have good performance confidence in all areas of your game, you will be amazed by the sport's sudden simplicity. You may even have moments when you feel certain you will never play poorly again!

Having this level of performance confidence in all areas of the game is rare and, unfortunately, impossible to retain. Most players find it more common to feel a lack of performance confidence in at least some aspect of their game. Then there are those especially challenging times when performance confidence in *all* areas is lost, leaving you wondering if you will ever play well again. While this is an extreme feeling, it is not uncommon—even among the top professionals. It is especially common after playing in exceptionally tough conditions with very poor results.

Still, no matter what the conditions, one of the realities of golf is that performance confidence always will ebb and flow. Most players only occasionally lose confidence in all areas of their game. It is more common to lose confidence in one area of your game as you find it in another.

The United States Golf Association is renowned for zapping performance confidence at the U.S. Open by the way it sets up its courses—narrow fairways, high rough, fast greens—to challenge its participants. This was especially true at the 1992 U.S. Open at Pebble Beach. And beyond the difficult course setup, things were made even more troublesome by the cool and blustery conditions during the tournament. More than the usual number of players left this event having shot scores in the 80s and with much lower performance confidence than when they arrived.

One such player was PGA Tour veteran Dan Forsman. He arrived at Pebble Beach in the midst of his tenth and best year on Tour, and his performance confidence was high since he had made the cut and played well in recent PGA Tour events. Since he had grown up in the San Francisco Bay Area, Dan viewed the 1992 Open at Pebble Beach as sort of a homecoming. But after shooting in the 80s and barely making the cut in front of family and friends, both Dan's performance and personal confidence were shattered.

Dan bravely rebounded to finish in a tie for sixtieth, but left the event feeling a need to go home to rebuild his performance confidence. Making time to regroup mentally and physically rather than forcing himself to play without it, Dan quickly recovered. Within two months, he'd won his fourth Tour title, in a playoff at the Buick Open.

Even the very experienced Senior Tour players are prone to lose all confidence in a single event. In the 1998 Las Vegas Senior Classic, considered by many participants and wives as a great tournament and a fun week enhanced by the city's hospitality, food, and entertainment, a number of players left the event wondering what had hit them. As strong winds gusted over the golf course, the fun was replaced by frustration, and performance confidence was replaced with lingering self-doubts.

Al Geiberger was one of these players. But in spite of some very high scores and considerable embarrassment, Al never gave up. The following week, in Birmingham, Alabama, at the Bruno's Memorial Classic, he realized he had some problems that were related to changes he'd made to compensate for the wind at the Las Vegas Senior Classic. His fundamentals, his famous tempo, and even his posture were subconsciously altered in his effort to play in the winds. Now he was in the very difficult position of trying to compete with little to no performance confidence.

After some discussion with us, Al agreed that his path back included (1) changing some bad habits of thought to improve his personal confidence and (2) putting in plenty of quality, structured practice—perhaps even a lesson on basics from his long-time instructor, Jim Blakely—to regain his performance confidence. Al also practiced with a long time friend and fan, Vince Jiminez, who understood and reminded Al of the basics of his great swing. Soon he had rebuilt his performance confidence and could return to playing well.

THE IMPORTANCE OF CONFIDENCE FOR COMPETITIVE GOLF

If you have played golf for a while you already know that it can be brutal on confidence. But the endless array of physical and mental challenges faced by golfers makes confidence one of the most important traits for peak performance and, as we have said, one of the most difficult to maintain. Yet, doing so is vital because of the many ways confidence contributes to the quality of your play.

Having confidence in yourself and your game allows you to get the most out of your skills; to play without the inhibiting, self-conscious concerns about what others think of you or your game; and to separate your identity from your game so that you can respect yourself in spite of poor play.

Let's examine the confidence of the champions in this sport. Champions walk, think, and talk with a level of confidence far above that of the average person. Whether they always feel it or not, they strive to project confidence in the ways they move and carry themselves, in the ways they think of themselves before and during competition, and in the ways they talk to themselves and others. More specifically, champions do the following:

- They seek to dwell on their strengths and involve themselves with things they can control rather than on weaknesses and things outside their control.
- They refuse to let self-doubts keep them from confidently swinging the club or stroking the ball to the best of their abilities.
- They channel mental energies into the process of confidently focusing on the shot at hand rather than wasting mental energies wrestling with concerns about how their swing or how their play will be perceived by others.
- They find every opportunity to compliment them-

selves on their skills, luck, or play to help counter the confidence-draining aspects of the game.

○ When they hit bad shots or play bad holes or rounds, they quickly look for the positive lessons to carry into their next play.

Now let's look at players with average-to-low confidence. Such players often display their lack of confidence with drooped shoulders; lowered chins; shuffling feet; or hyper, unsettled, and fidgety behavior. Seldom acknowledging it, the thoughts of these players are commonly negative, filled with dread, worry, or anticipation of poor play. Self-talk is critical and discouraging with regard to themselves, their circumstances, or their play. Without full awareness, their imagery often drifts to visions of how they do not want to play rather than how they do want to hit a shot. More specifically, players with average-to-low confidence do the following:

○ They dwell on their weaknesses and involve themselves with things they cannot control. This quickly becomes habitual, and the related bad thoughts and behaviors inhibit their play.

○ They let self-doubt and apprehension force them into steering, guiding, and forcing shots, rather than confidently swinging the club or stroking the ball.

○ They channel mental energies into second-guessing their abilities as well as worrying about poor results and how they will be perceived by others, rather than confidently focusing on the shot at hand and committing to what they can control.

○ They will give in to urges to berate themselves or their play and are oblivious to opportunities to compliment themselves on their skills, their luck, or their successes.

○ They take bad shots, bad rounds or criticism of their play personally. Poor play can negatively affect mood and attitude for hours or even days, negating any ability to learn from their mistakes.

If you recognize any of these tendencies, your next step is to determine whether your weakness is in personal confidence, performance confidence, or a combination of the two. The following charts will help. They describe the extremes of confidence and apprehension for personal and performance confidence. Estimate where you score on all items relative to the one-to-ten scale.

What Are Your Tendencies

Compare your tendencies to those listed in this simple chart. Keep in mind that 1 represents someone who is extremely confident; 10 represents someone who is extremely apprehensive; and 5 to 6 represents someone who is "average" in confidence. Estimate at which point of the scale you might score on this trait based on an average of *your* personal and golfing tendencies, then circle that number. Performance confidence is rated separately.

The champions are either confident or continually working on building personal confidence so that they maintain a healthy love of and appreciation for themselves. Performance

---

PERSONAL CONFIDENCE

Confident   **Apprehensive**

1	2	3	4	5	6	7	8	9	10

PERSONAL TENDENCIES:

Self-assured	Feels self-doubt
Secure	Insecure
Accepts compliments graciously	Uncomfortable with compliments
Values own qualities	Does not value own qualities

GOLFING TENDENCIES:

Positive self-talk	Negative self-talk
Accepts mistakes	Dwells on mistakes
Believes in abilities	Constantly questions abilities
Play has little influence on mood	Play greatly influences mood
Supportive of self	Hard on self

PERFORMANCE CONFIDENCE									
Confident									**Apprehensive**
1	**2**	**3**	**4**	**5**	**6**	**7**	**8**	**9**	**10**

GOLFING TENDENCIES:

Sure of fundamentals	Unsure of fundamentals
Sure of mental abilities	Unsure of mental abilities
Sure of physical abilities	Unsure of physical abilities
Trusts equipment	Does not trust in equipment

confidence fluctuates for everyone—the champions persistently organize their practice to build, maintain, and/or regain confidence in all aspects of their games.

Player Examples

Some of the top players are fortunate in that they come to the game of golf already equipped with strong personal confidence. Paul Azinger is a dramatic example of someone whose strong personal confidence fueled a remarkable perseverance through many levels of golf. Even though he started playing the game at the age of five, he was unable to break 40 for nine holes until he was a senior in high school. But he persevered, even trying to get a major college scholarship with a strong right-hand swing that many felt would not hold up. His perseverance continued when he turned pro. He got his Tour card, kept his Tour card, finally won a tournament, and then won a major. His greatest challenge, however, has been rediscovering his form after a fight with cancer.

Many players, on the other hand, come to golf with average-to-below-average confidence that must be strengthened at every opportunity. Some players who have very successfully demonstrated this ability include Jim Dent, Doug Martin, Mark McCumber, and Jackie Gallagher-Smith.

Let's start the process for improving your own *personal confidence* by determining your personal confidence rating. Answer the following questions using the point values below.

1: Always   2: Often   3: Sometimes   4: Seldom   5: Never

___ A. I often find fault with the things I do.

___ B. I am more likely to imagine what I do not want to happen than what I do want to happen.

___ C. I tend to question my abilities.

___ D. I feel self-conscious about how others view my abilities.

___ E. I feel disappointed or frustrated with myself.

___ F. My self-talk is more likely to be negative, destructive, and discouraging than it is to be positive, constructive, and encouraging.

_____ Total x 2 ÷ 6 = _____ Personal Confidence Rating

If you rated yourself 8 or higher, your personal confidence is strong and well suited to handle the ups and downs of your *golf* game. If you rated lower than 8, your personal confidence is probably weak enough to compromise your abilities as a golfer, and you should start working on your personal confidence immediately.

The techniques suggested here have proven helpful to many in strengthening personal confidence. They are not meant to replace a possible need for personal counseling but rather to initiate and facilitate change.

GOLFPSYCH TECHNIQUE: Improving Personal Confidence

"Confidence is the element I have to have if I am going to win. Sometimes I can win when I don't hit the ball well off the tee or if my short game isn't working, but if I'm not confident about what I'm doing, I'm not going to play well."

Lee Janzen

This technique involves a number of simple and effective steps you can take to begin strengthening your personal confidence. These steps are intended to increase awareness of inhibiting thoughts and to reduce your preoccupation with them. But remember, you are changing thinking habits, and as it would be with changing physical habits, it will take time and persistence to achieve.

Affirmations: These are compliments you bestow on yourself. Confident people freely and easily affirm themselves, while people with low personal confidence find it a difficult task that can feel awkward and even uncomfortable.

We often ask participants in our seminars and workshops to list five qualities they truly value about themselves. People with low confidence are lucky to eke out one or two items in the allotted time, sometimes scrunching their faces with discomfort as they try. The very confident participants frequently and easily provide even more than the requested five affirmations, in part because affirmations are an integral part of their daily thoughts. You can condition yourself to do more of the same with these steps.

Begin creating a list of your own affirmations. Compile at least fifty items that positively describe your strengths and good qualities with respect to personality, values, skills, accomplishments, looks, and so on. If you find the task overwhelming, challenge yourself to identify one or more per day over a period of several weeks. Suggestions from others are acceptable only if you also truly believe they are attributes.

Then take a few minutes each day to review your list. Choose at least one item and reflect on some recent evidence of that strength. For example, if the affirmation is patience, reflect on a recent demonstration of patience on the golf course, in traffic, or with a family member. Throughout the day, look for opportunities to mentally give yourself compliments. For example, privately compliment your own honesty by acknowledging you let a cashier know you received too much change.

Be prepared to accept affirmations and compliments from others graciously, without sarcasm or discrediting statements. For example, if someone compliments you on your swing, graciously accept; resist an urge to identify flaws and shortcomings or to question that person's ability to judge a golf swing.

Thought checks: As we have said, low self-confidence is re-inforced by bad habits of thought. But just as we have the ability to change physical habits, we also have the ability to change mental habits. In both cases, change starts with aware-ness. Thought checks will help you gain greater awareness and understanding of the bad habits of thought that fuel your low self-confidence.

A thought check involves taking a few conscious mo-ments to assess the quality of your thoughts. Are they produc-tive and positive, such as offering you positive solutions and compliments, or are they destructive and negative, such as second-guessing and berating? Challenge yourself to do thought checks at various times of day, especially in those sit-uations where you feel your confidence is at its lowest, such as around certain people, dealing with certain responsibilities, pondering certain problems, and so on. Your goal in using thought checks is to identify and change bad habits of thought related to negative self-talk and faulty thinking.

Once your thought checks have helped you identify habits of negative self-talk, its time to change those habits. Your first objective is to counter every negative thought with a positive one. If, for example, you feel angst because you hit a shot well but used the wrong club, give yourself a couple of seconds to react, then compliment yourself on how well you hit the shot.

Your next objective is to get out of past tense as quickly as possible. This involves intercepting the self-talk that begins with "I should have" or "I could have." Instead, opt for self-talk that is more positive and future-oriented. For example, you can berate yourself for not having fully committed to your shot before you hit it, or you can confidently assure your-self that on your next shot you will fully commit to your club and your target. Always choose the latter.

Faulty thinking: Changing negative self-talk is much more

difficult, however, for those who, usually without realizing it, have habits of reasoning, deducing, and thinking of others and themselves in ways that are highly illogical.

Faulty thinking is detrimental to confidence because it wastes considerable mental energy; it interferes with good, peaceful focus; it can be totally distracting; and it is almost always negative, unproductive, and inhibiting.

Here are some examples of faulty thinking. Do you recognize any of them in yourself or in someone you know?

- *Mind-reading:* Some players spend a lot of time wondering and assuming what other people are thinking of them, their games, looks, abilities, clothing, hairstyle, or any other personal attributes. An example in golf would be the man on the first tee who finds his attention is not focused on tempo, commitment, picture, and feel, but rather on who is watching and what they will see and think about him. Or it could be the golfer who, when playing or practicing near someone with a lower handicap or greater reputation, can only concern himself with how they are being perceived by that player.
- *All or nothing:* Players with low confidence frequently think of themselves in all-or-nothing terms. For example, if they made six great putts and three poor putts, they are more likely to state at the end of a round that they "putted terrible today" instead of "I putted great today with the exception of three difficult ones." If they play well overall but have one bad hole, all-or-nothing thinkers will declare they are terrible golfers.
- *Magnification:* Similar to all-or-nothing thinking, magnification leads players to quickly draw some dramatic, negative deductions about themselves and their games. Magnifiers see themselves at the extreme of any problem they encounter. For example, after a bad round he is likely to harbor fears that his game is falling apart. If

he plays poorly on the first hole, he is sure he will play poorly the rest of the day. If someone criticizes one shot, he feels he must be a terrible golfer.

○ *Defensiveness:* Many with low confidence tend to be very defensive and take much of what happens around them very personally. If they are warned about slow play, they are certain they are being harassed. If other players move or talk during their swings, they are convinced it is intentional. If they get an unlucky bounce, the gods are against them. They allow people and circumstances to negatively influence their personal confidence.

So what can be done to solve faulty thinking? First, make a list of all the issues that negatively affected your mood in the past several days. Write down your thoughts related to those issues. Where possible, compare your thoughts to the examples of faulty thinking above and label the ones you feel you experienced. Now try to write alternative thoughts that you would consider to be more rational and productive in relation to each issue. Do this exercise several times a week until you can catch and replace faulty thinking as it occurs. On the golf course, you will find it very helpful to use the bubble exercise described in Chapter 5 to detach and reduce your involvement with faulty thoughts.

The suggestions above are meant to increase self-awareness and strengthen your thinking habits. If these techniques don't work, you will likely benefit from good personal counseling. With the assistance of a qualified and licensed therapist, you will be able to resolve past issues and current conflicts, change subconscious perceptions of yourself, and identify possible biochemical influences that compromise your personal confidence.

Strengthening your personal confidence may well be the best thing you will ever do for yourself as a golfer and a person.

GOLFPSYCH TECHNIQUE:
Improving Performance Confidence

Even with great personal confidence, performance confidence can be fleeting. By the same token, a lack of personal confidence can undermine the greatest performance confidence in the world. The steps we recommend here will help you maintain this important trait.

First, let's identify areas of low, moderate, and high performance confidence. Using a simple one-to-ten scale, with 1 representing very low confidence and 10 representing very high confidence, periodically rate your performance confidence in these playing areas.

Low Confidence							**High Confidence**		
1	**2**	**3**	**4**	**5**	**6**	**7**	**8**	**9**	**10**
Driver									
Fairway woods									
Long irons									
Middle irons									
Short irons									
Chipping									
Bunker shots									
Putting									

Note: The higher your skills level, the more you will benefit from rating specific types of shots within these groupings, such as use of specific clubs, abilities on certain grasses, effectiveness on various lies, abilities in certain conditions, or effectiveness hitting various partial shots.

As we have mentioned, fluctuation in performance confidence is natural. But as you periodically rate your confidence in these areas, you may begin to find a specific area or areas that have been low for a while. Make it your goal to sort out why, so that you can take definite steps toward change.

This is precisely what Paul Azinger has had to do since

the diagnosis and treatment of his cancer. Before he was diagnosed with a lymphoma in his shoulder blade at the end of 1993, Paul's five years of hard work had helped him develop extreme performance confidence. He was finishing his best year on tour, with twelve top-ten finishes, three wins, and a second-place ranking on the year's money list, with $1,458,456.

The following year his performance confidence was obliterated. Surgery, chemotherapy, and radiation allowed Paul to compete in only four events. He made the cut in two and finished 242nd on the money list. As he began to rebuild his performance confidence in 1995, Paul recognized that there were three areas upon which he needed to focus: his mind, his mechanics, and his equipment.

STRONG MENTAL SKILLS

"I never had to think about my rhythm and timing. I always had it, but I lost it."

Paul Azinger

We have found that when players with moderate to high skills begin working on their games, they should incorporate the mental game as soon as possible, especially when their games have been sabotaged by an injury or an illness. We suggest this because time after time we see that as the fundamentals of a strong mental game—commitment, visualization, tempo, rhythm, timing, feel—improve, so do the mechanics. Paul recognized this too. After having had to place so much emphasis on physically rehabilitating his upper body and mechanically rebuilding his swing, he realized—once he returned to the Tour—that he had gotten away from the use of his lower body and the *feel*, of his swing. In the past he'd always keyed on feel as opposed to mechanics, so recovering his lower body strength and his feel became his goal.

Dave Stockton provides a different but related example of recouping mental strength. The 1995 U.S. Senior Open was held at Congressional, outside Washington, D.C. Because it was a major and it was being staged at the sight of one of his PGA Championship wins, Dave felt an overwhelming desire to play well. As a result, he spent the two weeks prior to the tournament working especially hard on his physical skills so that he would be as prepared as possible for the event.

Dave and I spotted each other as he finished his first practice round at Congressional. He was visibly upset and frustrated. Ralph Cross, his long-time agent and friend, had just walked nine holes with him and explained that Dave was very unhappy with his game. Dave further explained that he was hitting the ball terribly and that he just could not get comfortable with his swing. He decided he needed an "attitude adjustment." We immediately sat down to discuss steps he might take to regain some of his usually good performance confidence.

Dave has always been a great feel player, as most great putters are. But like most golfers going into an important event, he has a tendency to overprepare the physical side of his game at the expense of the mental. His practice had been almost all mechanical, with little attention to touch, timing, and feel.

It was important for Dave now to reduce his emphasis on swing mechanics and tap into his natural and trained abilities by improving his mental strengths. This included getting back to the basics of the mental routine by committing to clubs and targets, visualizing his shots, and feeling a great tempo in his swing. Dave needed to forget mechanics and concentrate on the creative aspects of shot making. This would be his path to quickly regaining enough performance confidence to play his best with the physical skills he had at that time.

I suggested Dave go to the practice tee. He was to forget mechanics and instead pick a target, get very relaxed, and just hit different shots at that target simply by seeing his shot and feeling his tempo. One of Dave's favorite and effective ways of doing this, which he developed during his years of corporate outing demonstrations, is to have someone call the type of shot they want him to hit as he starts his takeaway, then challenge himself to create that shot with the downswing. The spontaneity requires him to create rather than manufacture the desired shot.

Dave and Ralph headed for the practice tee. I agreed to join them in ten minutes to help out. I wasn't needed. I arrived to find Dave and Ralph sporting large smiles. Dave was visibly more relaxed with better tempo and a better stroke. He was hitting his best shots of the day. Already he was committed to a good mental routine and was more confident with his swing.

Building performance confidence can indeed start by correcting swing mechanics, but you risk spending unproductive time and making unnecessary changes if you do not first address your mental problems.

High tension is the perfect example. High tension creates faulty swing mechanics that are often cured with a more relaxed body and mind. We have seen numerous advanced players treat symptoms of mental weaknesses by putting in diligent hours, weeks, and months of hard work to incorporate physical changes only to return to competition with weak mental skills that still inhibit performance confidence.

So we strongly encourage you to make sure that at least the fundamentals of your mental game—particularly your mental routine—are strong before assessing, changing, and working on your physical skills.

STRONG PHYSICAL SKILLS

" . . . confidence derives only from efficient swing mechanics."

Jack Nicklaus

After rededicating himself to golf, Azinger at first found it difficult to put in the hours necessary to find his way back. This was partly because he'd developed an even greater appreciation for other things in his life, such as his family, his faith, and his fishing, which all played a role in his successful recovery. There was also some reluctance to put himself through some of the same rigors that somehow may have contributed to his illness. He'd been told, although he was not sure if it were true, that the high stress and the physical strains of playing pro golf had predisposed him to an onset of biological events that may have contributed to the growth of cancerous cells.

But after shooting an 82 at the 1996 Shell Houston Open, things changed. After telling his wife, Toni, that he had completely lost it and that he would never be good again, she told him, "You don't practice like you used to." She added that there was nothing wrong with not practicing the way he used to, but that if he didn't, then he shouldn't complain. He knew she was right.

With Toni's encouragement, and the support of Bill Western, a teaching professional, Paul committed himself to really work on his game. After hitting many balls—one day he hit 500 eight irons—Paul finally started to feel some of the old positions, see the right trajectories of his shots, and hear the right sounds when he hit the ball. Rounding out his efforts were suggestions from someone who knew his swing better than anyone: his long-time teaching professional, John Redman.

Your ability to hit reasonably predictable shots is vital to your performance confidence. Keep in mind that having a perfect swing is not as important as having a swing you trust and can count on under pressure. Getting this often requires the assistance of a qualified teaching professional who has a good eye for your swing and can communicate in a style to which you relate. It's not always easy to find someone, but it's worth the effort.

You should try to establish a relationship with an instructor who can teach you the fundamentals in a style that matches your personality and your game. Use him or her to help monitor your progress and get you back in position when you inevitably stray from the basics. Even at the peak of his career, Jack Nicklaus made a point of visiting his lifelong teacher, Jack Grout, at least once a year. Together they would check out his grip, setup, and all the fundamentals, making corrections to ensure Jack's practice increased his confidence.

Your personality will influence the quantity and type of practice that best suits you. For example, feel players seem to prefer less practice and more play, with their practice emphasizing touch, timing, and feel. Mechanical players seem to prefer more practice and less play, with their practice emphasizing drills and positions. To be honest, most players can benefit from including a bit more of what they least prefer.

Two tempting but bad habits most players with low performance confidence will face are: overpracticing to the point of fatigue or poor concentration and allocating most of their practice to areas of their games in which they are already confident. But in building and maintaining performance confidence, it is vital to organize quality practice for the areas of your game that need it the most. Quality practice is designed to improve your weakest skills in the most effective way.

EQUIPMENT

"The effectiveness of a golf club usually results much more from its influence on a player's mind than on his actual golf swing."

Jack Nicklaus

As confidence in your physical skills improves, you will be able to assess whether changes in your equipment will further strengthen your performance confidence. Players have the most performance confidence when they feel good about their clubs, and there are several reasons they do:

○ The clubs fit in terms of length, loft, lie, and stiffness and flex point of the shafts.

○ The player hits the "sweet spot" consistently.
○ A club or putter looks and feels good in the player's hands.
○ The player hits shots he likes in terms of height, shape, and spin reasonably consistently.

Advances in the technology of golf equipment over the years have been remarkable, to the advantage of both amateurs and professionals. Paying too much attention to equipment, however, often does not solve the real problem and can be detrimental to performance confidence at any level of play. Tinkering can become a habit, and continually changing equipment affords no time to build confidence. As Lee Trevino would say, "It's not the arrow, it's the Indian."

In spite of his frustration, Paul Azinger resisted falling into a pattern of tinkering with his equipment to find his confidence. Although he changed irons as part of an endorsement agreement, he believed in and continued to use the same driver and wedges. Feeling as though he was hitting all his shots too high or that he was pull-hooking them, Paul refuted the opinion of some that his resistance to changing equipment was hurting his game. He was convinced his challenges were mental and physical, rather than equipment-related, and he wanted to confirm or reject this suspicion before changing equipment. By 1998, Paul had played twenty-two events and had climbed back up to fiftieth on the money list, without changing his equipment.

To ensure your equipment helps build your personal confidence, you should make sure that your clubs are properly fitted and that they look and feel good to you. That done, commit to your equipment for two months or until you feel you have given yourself every chance to gain performance confidence through your mental and physical skills.

During this trial period, evaluate your performance with each club and with the whole set. Then if you feel you should change your equipment, do so because of your own evaluation and not on a whim or suggestion from a friend. And certainly not because of an ad you saw in a magazine or on television or because a favorite Tour pro is playing a certain model.

PERSONALIZATION:
Texas Wesleyan University Golf Team

In January of 1995, Dan Forsman recommended us to Mike Skipper, an alumnus of Texas Wesleyan University. Being an avid supporter and generous benefactor of the university's golf team, Mike excitedly saw another way to assist the team and its coach, Bobby Cornett.

When he approached Bobby, Mike was met with enthusiasm. Bobby is a strong competitive golfer himself and readily recognizes the importance of a strong mental game, not only for his own golf game and those of his team members, but also for his other athletic endeavors, which include nationally competitive table tennis and long distance running.

Mike initiated the call and made arrangements for the entire team (ten players and coach) to be tested. We discussed and planned to meet as a group to review their results, set personal and team goals, problem-solve, and initiate activities to build team cohesion in a one day meeting here at Tapatio Springs Resort.

Before the team arrived, we reviewed the test scores to begin assessing their primary needs. Our first impression was that Bobby had recruited and assembled what appeared to be a pretty cohesive group. Most were at or above average in self-discipline with only a couple's test results showing the need for considerable help in setting priorities and organizing time—vital for college players balancing golf, academics, and social time. Most players tested were shown to be conscientious, or likely to comply with his rules for the team, including the four-mile runs Bobby asks his players to make twice a week. Except for a couple, the group tested to be average or a little above average in abstract thinking. The implication of this was that most should be able to handle academics, assimilate new information about their games fairly quickly (including what we were planning to teach them), and effectively think their way around the golf course. Bobby had assembled a team that, except for one, was also rather emotionally stable, without huge personal issues in need of resolving before they could focus on golf or grades.

Two major areas stood out as we looked for ways to strengthen the Texas Wesleyan Golf team as a whole. With the exception of two players, the group was made up of extroverts. This trait (along with being enthusiastic, which they *all* tested to be, including their coach) made them a really fun group to be around. But the extroversion implied to us that most of the team would have considerable difficulty concentrating unless they had been taught skills to effectively narrow their focus over the ball under any circumstance.

The second major area that stood to weaken the team as a whole was confidence. We knew from the scores that only two players tested to have the above average personal confidence we look for in competitive golf. Performance confidence fluctuates, and we would assess that in our meeting. The personal confidence was more of a concern at this point so we wanted not only to verify and explain its effect on their performances but also to provide them with steps for change.

The first half of our day involved watching the team play so that we could assess the players' tendencies, especially with regard to focus and confidence. The latter, and the topic of this chapter, we assess largely by mannerisms and self-talk. The second half of the day we spent in a meeting room. As we explained and taught the eight champion traits, we queried the players regarding what they perceived as their problems. Our concerns about confidence (among numerous other things, including poor focus) were confirmed. Players described things like: questioning their abilities; often seeing what they do not want to happen; feeling self-conscious around other good players; frequently feeling like the under-dog; being flooded with doubt and negative thoughts over the ball; calling themselves names; becoming easily discouraged after a bad shot, hole, or round; or feeling and being affected by the effects of a poor tournament for days or weeks following.

We had the players begin a list of affirmations. They were to add to and review this list daily. We encouraged them to use thought checks to frequently check the quality of their thoughts, replacing negative and inhibiting thoughts with positive and encouraging thoughts.

We challenged them to talk to themselves as they would a friend, both on and off the golf course. We also encouraged them to practice and get very good at using adversity as a cue to convert negative experiences into positive thoughts. For example, after a bad shot they were to resist old habits of berating themselves; rather, they were to use the experience as a cue or reminder to commit to a great mental routine on their next shot. Bad shots, holes, rounds, and tournaments were to be perceived as "lessons" and a natural part of their progression. They should expect to experience one step back for every two steps forward in the pursuit of their goals. They were to endeavor to learn the most about themselves and what they could improve upon from their worst experiences.

For many we also recommended the bubble exercise to help them "push out" any thoughts that could take away confidence, including "mind reading" other people, self-criticism, questioning abilities, etc.

The team fully participated in all aspects of the meeting, relaying personal experiences, asking questions, offering suggestions to one another and agreeing to support each other in their efforts and setting team goals.

Bobby eagerly accepted the challenge of doing a follow-up with individuals regarding their individual goals, team goals, pre-round strategy sessions and post-round reviews, etc.

The efforts and perseverance of the team and coach combined to provide some dramatic results. They are described in this letter from the coach.

November 28, 1995

Dear Deborah and Jon:

I've been wanting to write before now but I am just now finding the time. Where to start? Something sticks out as I look back over our college season from our session in Boerne, Texas, to date. Something that Deborah said late that night in February, "Be prepared to take two steps forward and one step back."

I think that's how our team as well as several players individually has reacted to our encounter with GolfPsych.

Right now, ten months after our first session, we are ranked #1 in the Nation (NAIA) and have won our last three tournaments. We won the last by 29 shots over the second place team (copy enclosed), with the entire field being NCAA Division I and II schools. We are getting better all the time.

In this last tournament, Steve Galko won by 8 shots, scoring 6 under in very windy conditions (first two rounds) on a difficult Arnold Palmer design. That was the same Steve that shot 69 to lead our first collegiate event after our February session and followed it with an 82 to finish ninth on a quality 7100 yd. course. Same Steve that opened the National Championship Tournament with 80–80. He followed that with 73–72 at crunch time for a tie for 48th. Same Steve that plans to run 26.2 miles on February 24, 1996, in the Cowtown Marathon and has already done 13 miles in training. Same Steve who, last week, was named Outstanding Economics and Finance Student at our school. Hmm? Does anyone else see something happening here?

Or Jonathan Phillips, who hasn't been a top-five player for us in three years. About three months after our session last February he stated that your session "changed his life." He is currently playing a solid #5 and his best golf ever at Wesleyan, finishing one shot out of third in our last tournament. In October he led the Texas Intercollegiate after 36 holes with rounds of 72 and 68. He finished with a 77 for fifth. Let's see: two steps forward, one step back.

Or Billy Willenberg, who last February was in his tenth semester of his fourth college to attend and to that point has done very little that was noteworthy with his college golf. He also told me that your session changed his life. There is evidence to that effect: from that point on in 17 tournament rounds he averaged 75.59, significantly better than his previous college golf. He almost pulled off something that I hadn't considered possible prior to his last semester's play: All-American. A final round 76 in the National Championship knocked him out by two shots. Still this was his best college tournament ever! Enclosed find a small clipping about his summer after an attempt at qualifying for the U.S. Amateur. Billy started triple-bogey, bogey, triple-bogey on the first three holes and still qualified by scoring 76 in the morning round followed by a 68. In Newport, Rhode Island, he didn't make the top 64 for match play. Two forward/one back.

Team-wise after February 1995 we finished second in San Antonio, third in Dallas, second in Fort Worth, second in Wichita, Kansas, and then a breakthrough win at Pine Needles, North Carolina, with a 285 final round. Pine Needles is the site of the 1996 U.S. Women's Open. Richard Noon, a freshman, made thirteen birdies in two rounds on this quality golf course and finished fifth.

Our HOT Conference (Heart of Texas) victory earned an automatic birth to the National Championship with a #1 National ranking. This had me a little worried as I wasn't sure how the players would react to this built-in expectation. Unfortunately, I think it affected our play in the beginning. Two steps forward/one back.

After two rounds we were in eighth place, twelve shots back. After that round we wanted to loosen things up so we rented a VCR and the movie *Caddieshack* and everyone laughed for a couple of hours before lights out. Third round—low round of the day, we moved up to fourth, five shots behind.

Since the movie thing helped and now *we* were the underdogs, we decided to keep the VCR another day and rent the movie *Rudy.*

The last day we started at 8:00 A.M. and got three players on the course before the rain and lightning hit. Three inches.

The leading team's coach didn't think we would get the round in but our players expected to play and I reinforced that thought. Six hours after our tee time, we started again. Richard Noon and I on the #2, second shot, a tough par four with greenside creek in front.

Richard: "I'm thinking 4 or 5 iron."
Coach: "Gee, I was thinking 7 iron."
         "Surely it's going to fly out of that lie, maybe
         6 but that's plenty."

It didn't. Two feet short of perfect but in the water.

Coach: "My bad!"
Richard: Smile.

He dropped into a bad lie and got the next one on the fringe barely over the water 50 feet from the hole. Made it for bogey! Hmm?

On #4, a par four dogleg right around a lake, Billy drives it in the hazard. Jamie misses the green left in a really bad spot but Texas wedges it to ten feet and makes it for par. Billy hits a 4 iron to 25 feet and makes it for par. Hmm?

After I saw that I knew we had a chance. Rob Lang's 71 in the last round along with Jamie Drysdale's All-American performance for tenth place helped us to the closest finish in the NAIA history. A one-shot win over West Florida. Wow!

We should have been exhausted but we weren't. What a thrill. The enclosed picture was taken right after the guys found out they had won. Kind of hard to fake smiles like that. Thank you for your influence on these young men's lives. I know for a fact that each one came away from your efforts a better equipped player and person.

Sincerely,
Bobby Cornett
Head Golf Coach
Texas Wesleyan University

Seven

Self-Sufficiency

○

△

"A competitive golfer has to make more decisions in one day than some people face in one week."

Leonard Thompson

Part of golf's allure is the endless and varied decisions that must be made as a player continually assesses and strategizes. To many, this can be mentally stimulating, but for others—those who find it difficult to make decisions—golf can be mentally exhausting. Ironically, the greater the player's intellect and understanding of the game, the more overwhelming the decision-making can be.

Champions, not surprisingly, are above average in self-sufficiency and very good at making many difficult decisions, even under pressure. Their self-sufficiency, as we refer to it here, involves not only an ability to make decisions but an actual preference for doing so.

For some of them, self-sufficiency and decision-making come quite easily, while for others they may take considerable effort. There also is a smaller percentage of players who have relatively too much self-sufficiency for golf, meaning it is unlikely they will seek advice or instruction from others. Too much or too little can compromise competitive skills. And both appear to be influenced by our past and present circumstances.

Psychologists have determined that self-sufficiency is largely learned through life experiences, both as a child and as an adult. So while genetics plays a small role, you can increase your self-sufficiency by initiating steps for change.

Many of the circumstances that determine our self-sufficiency are rooted in childhood. Experts in personality have found that most people with low self-sufficiency, also referred to as "group orientation," had parents who either indulged and spoiled them; who did not encourage and reward their independence; or who were unable to provide their basic dependency needs, making them more "needy" than normal. Those with extremely high self-sufficiency were found to have felt secure in their early home environments; were not overly protected; and had parents who encouraged healthy initiative. Players who are extreme in this trait usually found some type of security in their early home environments where decision-making was encouraged. For example, they likely felt loved and protected by their parents (or parent), but were given considerable opportunity to exercise free will—picking clothes, selecting friends, deciding on what food to eat, and such.

Even though they do not always make the correct decisions, champion golfers know the importance of making a decision before executing a shot. Sometimes it is difficult to feel decisive, such as when playing in strong gusty winds. But the best players strive to commit themselves to at least 90 percent of their shots no matter what the conditions. This is not to say that the best players do not question themselves and their choices, because they do. Rather, they are adamant about not hitting shots before they fully commit to some choice. As we have said before, and as we often remind our players, you will get more out of your game committing to wrong decisions than you will by hitting shots when you aren't committed to the right decisions.

Making and committing to decisions is at least as important in some ways as improving your swing. In some ways, it is even more important since it can influence your preparation. Self-sufficiency influences how much you practice, what you practice, and your ability to secure the best assistance for your game. More specifically, above average self-sufficiency enables the champion to make decisions and commit to the following items:

Fundamentals: A highly self-sufficient player chooses and commits to techniques that are best suited to his game. While he is open to suggestions from qualified teachers, he is not easily influenced to take the advice of everyone who offers it.

Equipment: He remains true to his equipment but also stays on top of technological changes. He resists vacillation, and when put in a position to make a decision about his equipment, he does so without being heavily swayed by others.

Course management: He determines a plan for managing the course and remains committed to it, regardless of how others choose to play it. He's adaptable but decisive in handling necessary changes that he decides to make.

Clubs, targets, and types of shots: He strives to be as fully committed as possible to clubs, targets, and types of shots before striking the ball and resists being strongly influenced by the choices of others.

Practice: He independently determines a purpose for his practice and organizes it to meet his goal for the session, the day, the week, or the year.

Now let's look at players with too little self-sufficiency.

Players with less self-sufficiency find golf more fun when it's played with a partner or as part of a team. Including, or even seeking, someone else to be responsible in decision-making comes quite naturally to this golfer.

Self-Sufficiency   163

Golfers with less self-sufficiency will try to organize most of their practice and play with either a teacher or friend. Some even prefer that someone else tell them when to practice, what to practice, how to play a course, or even how to hit particular shots. A number of the players who've worked with us have done so because they were finding it difficult to make the transition from team-oriented college golf to professional golf. They felt overwhelmed with the self-sufficiency required for managing their own time, planning their own schedules, traveling alone, organizing their own travel and practice, not to mention maintaining and adapting their games for the various courses and conditions.

Players with too little self-sufficiency are likely to feel indecisive about some or all of the following:

Fundamentals: The player with little self-sufficiency looks to others for all direction because he has not developed or does not trust his own abilities to sort out swing problems.

Equipment: Others can easily convince him that equipment should be changed. He may choose equipment based on what is being used by peers or he may accept too much advice regarding clubs, shafts, grips, balls, and so forth.

Course management: He too easily questions his decision-making abilities. He often abandons his own strategy for playing the course to adopt strategies of other players.

Clubs, targets, and types of shots: This golfer does not have his own game plan or abandons his to choose clubs or targets being used by others. If he is using a caddie, he will allow him to make too many of the decisions.

Practice: He finds it difficult to decide on a practice regimen or schedule that benefits his game. He can easily make socialization more important than the quality of his practices.

Now let's examine those with the opposite situation.

Players with extremely high self-sufficiency can encounter problems of a different type. They are too resistant to ask for help, advice, or support from others. In times of stress, very self-sufficient players are more likely to withdraw and try to sort out problems on their own. They are also more likely to suppress problems, rather than talk them out, thereby magnifying their impact.

Here are the signs of extreme self-sufficiency:

Fundamentals: The extremely self-sufficient golfer will take longer than others to work out problems because he prefers to sort things out on his own.

Equipment: He may reject all suggestions regarding equipment, preferring to gather his own information and draw his own conclusions.

Game plan: He is much less likely to discuss strategy with others, thereby losing possible advantages gained through their experiences or insights.

Clubs, targets, and types of shots: He is likely to decline the suggestions of a caddie, teacher, or coach—even when he needs the assistance.

THE CHAMPION GOLFER

You do not need to be above average in self-sufficiency to enjoy golf socially, but the more competitive you are, the more important your decision-making skills become. To help you understand the level of self-sufficiency needed for peak performance in golf, we suggest you rate your tendencies toward group orientation or self-sufficiency.

What Are Your Tendencies?

Compare your tendencies to those listed in this simple chart. Keep in mind that 1 represents someone who is extremely group oriented; 10 represents someone who is extremely self-sufficient; and 5 to 6 represents someone who can go either way—lead or follow. Estimate at which point of this scale you might score on this trait based on *your* personal and golfing tendencies, then circle that number.

Group Oriented							Self-Sufficient		
1	2	3	4	5	6	7	8	9	10

PERSONAL TENDENCIES:

Prefers group decision-making	Prefers making own decisions
Works well on committees	Works well alone
Open to suggestions	Resists suggestions
Will ask for help	Avoids asking for help

GOLFING TENDENCIES:

Gets too much instruction	Gets too little instruction
Difficulty making own decisions	Great at making own decisions
Too quick to accept help	Stubbornly refuses help
Over-reliance on caddies	Under-use of caddies

You do not need to be above average in self-sufficiency to enjoy social golf, though the more competitive you are, the more important your decision-making skills become.

The champions are above average, though seldom extreme, in self-sufficiency. They not only like making their own decisions, they prefer it. Yet, they do leave themselves somewhat open to suggestions or help.

Player Examples

There are many group-oriented players who have learned to be more self-sufficient, among them Homero Blancas, Doug Tewell, Amy Read, DeWitt Weaver, Dan Forsman, Don Pooley, John Schroeder, and Lori Tatum. Some, on the other hand, reach the professional level and find they do not enjoy being so self-sufficient. An example is Martha Richards-Freitag, from Hudson, Wisconsin. Because of her prowess in both golf and basketball at Stanford University, *USA Today* selected Martha as the "1988 Female Athlete-of-the-Year." As well as playing on the 1990 NCAA championship basketball team, Martha also was selected as a 1993 All-American and a 1993 First Team All PAC-10 in golf. Upon graduating, she won her LPGA card, making her eligible to compete on the Tour in 1995.

Martha is a driven, warm, conscientious, and organized competitor who is also group-oriented. Although she is a take-charge person, she does it in a team environment, so she found the individual-oriented aspects of the LPGA Tour much less enjoyable than the team efforts to which she was so accustomed. She made the decision to return to team sports as a college coach and has since found much happiness in a competitive outlet that also makes great use of her people-oriented and group-oriented skills.

The flip side involves players who are great decision-makers but often are slower to reach out for assistance or advice. But some have pushed themselves to seek assistance, most often to their advantage. Such players include Mike Hulbert, Hal Sutton, Scott Verplank, Emlyn Aubrey, Michael Bradley, Tom Byrum, Mark Calcavecchia, Robert Gamez, Bill Glasson, David Sutherland, Phil Blackmar, Cathy Gerring, Maggie Will, and Dale Eggeling.

Asking for help does not generally come easily to these players, but when they do seek help, they usually go to someone they deeply respect. This was the case with Phil Blackmar. Phil joined the Tour in 1985 and won twice within the next three years. In 1994, his career nosedived and he had to go back to the Tour's Qualifying School. Soon afterward, he realized that something had to be done to his approach, but he wasn't sure of the answer. So he turned to his wife, Carol.

Phil is well known among the touring professionals as one of the best fishermen on Tour—an honor not to be taken lightly. Carol simply suggested that if he put the same passion into his golf as he put into his fishing, he would see great rewards. He listened, and he did. In 1997, Phil surpassed his previous best earnings by nearly $400,000 and won his third event.

Would you long persist on your own as Phil did? Or would you have sought too much advice? The answer will be much clearer as you become more aware of low and high levels of self-sufficiency in golf: knowing your tendencies, you can then start maximizing or minimizing your self-sufficiency for peak performance.

HOW SELF-SUFFICIENT ARE YOU?

"It's important to be able to find things out on your own because when it comes down to the back nine at Augusta, it's Lee Janzen out there making the decisions."

Lee Janzen

To get a quick measure of your self-sufficiency, rate your tendencies by applying the following point values to these statements.

1: Always   2: Often   3: Sometimes   4: Seldom   5: Never

___ A. My decisions on how to play a hole, shot, or putt are influenced by how others choose to play the hole, shot, or putt.

___ B. I hit my putts still questioning my line or speed.

___ C. I execute shots without a full commitment to at least one of the following: my club, a definite target, or the type of shot I want to hit.

___ D. It is common for me to take advice from a variety of people, golf books, or magazines.

___ E. I am easily enticed to try new and different equipment.

___ F. I take total responsibility for my game, being my own teacher and correcting my own strokes and swings.

___ G. I find it uncomfortable to ask for help with my game.

___ H. I reject advice given by others regarding my equipment, my swing, and the way I manage the course.

___ I. I find it difficult to discuss my bad rounds with others.

_____ Total x 2 ÷ 9 = _____ Self-Sufficiency Rating

If you rated 8 or higher, your self-sufficiency appears to be suited to competitive golf. Remain open to new information and take steps for strengthening your play, but be sure decisions are ultimately your own—and that you're fully committed to them.

If you rated lower than 8 overall and your lowest ratings were on questions 1–5, you will likely improve your golf by learning to be more self-sufficient and decisive in your approach to practice and play.

If you were lower than 8 and your lowest ratings were on questions 6–9, your self-sufficiency might be extreme enough to inhibit your success with golf. Take a few steps to reduce the intensity of this trait.

MANAGING WHAT HARMS
GOOD DECISION-MAKING

It is not unusual for self-sufficiency to fluctuate, since weaknesses in other areas can reduce your ability to make decisions. Here are some of the many other factors that can reduce your decision-making skills along with descriptions and suggestions for strengthening each.

Low personal or performance confidence: Without confidence, it will be difficult to trust your own decisions no matter how good they are, leaving you looking for validation elsewhere. Suggestions: Rate your confidence in Chapter 6 and review the suggestions for strengthening personal and performance confidence. You can improve performance confidence by identifying specific aspects of your game that need improvement, establishing a plan for doing so, and practicing. You can improve personal confidence by changing some internal beliefs about yourself, improving your self-talk, and becoming more familiar with your strengths and attributes.

Tension: Golfers are typically unaware of rising tension until it is beyond control, but there are tell-tale signs. Your mind gets busier, for example. You feel less comfortable with your alignment and you're less trusting of first impressions, both of which make committing to your shots much more difficult. Suggestions: Read more about tension in Chapter 8 to learn techniques for managing physical and mental tension. Physical techniques include such things as deep breathing, shoulder rolls, and stretching. Mental techniques include thought-stopping, meditation, and positive imagery.

Emotional instability: If you experience high levels of emotions such as anger, fear, disappointment, excitement, frustration, and the like when you play, it's much more difficult to assess options rationally and make effective decisions. Suggestions: Review Chapter 3 to control your emotions better. You should emphasize managing your thoughts and taking mental breaks between shots. Keep in mind that unresolved personal issues make these tasks difficult.

Reduced mental alertness and fatigue: As with tension, few golfers are fully aware of reduced mental alertness and fatigue until its onset. Three clear indicators are indecisiveness, reduced visualization skills, and impatience. There can be many causes besides simply pushing too hard, including inadequate sleep, nutritional deficiencies, excessive worry, drugs, alcohol, medication, and low blood sugar. Suggestions: Begin with the obvious—take good care of yourself. Balance your life; improve your diet and sleeping habits; reduce or eliminate caffeine, nicotine, alcohol, and drugs; identify and change things in your life that are out of order. Players who notice a pattern of feeling less decisive after making the turn often are experiencing a drop in blood sugar. It is important for these golfers to eat a balanced meal before play and carry balanced snacks to eat on the course.

Once you start to address the problems that mimic low self-sufficiency, you will have a better idea of how self-sufficient you really are. And you will be ready to implement the following techniques to help you emulate a champion's self-sufficiency.

○ Practice making your own decisions on and off the course. When faced with choices, large or small, assess all available information and options before seeking assistance. You'll find that you will become more capable of making decisions.

○ Organize your practice sessions. Identify goals to meet during practice and identify the steps you must take to reach them.

○ "Journal" your golf. Many golfers have improved their decision-making skills by incorporating the simple task of keeping an account of their practice and play. This involves taking a few moments after each round to chronicle your current mental strengths and weaknesses and your current physical strengths and weaknesses. You can use a notebook, diary, personal planner, or computer to do this. Strengthening your physical weaknesses becomes your goal for practice. Strengthening your mental weaknesses becomes your goal for play. In addition to writing down your strengths and weaknesses, jot down your goals and make a few notes on how you can best accomplish them, such as choosing drills, devices, practice games, or lessons to address the physical weaknesses or, to address the mental ones, choosing definite targets, visualizing shots, and improving tempo.

DECISION-MAKING WITH A CADDIE

It is important to stay in charge when you employ a caddie. Even if your caddie is your parent, your friend, your sponsor, your boss, or even your spouse, you must be both committed to and responsible for your own decisions. A knowledgeable caddie can be a great asset to you in competition as he or she gathers needed information, points out things you may miss, and supports you in your decisions. But the caddie's input should not go beyond that. There may be instances in which you may be playing a course with which you're not familiar.

Even here the caddie should be a provider of information. If the caddie tells you, for example, to hit to a certain spot, determine why and input your knowledge about your own game before committing to the shot.

We see the greatest conflicts between self-sufficient, dominant players and self-sufficient, dominant caddies. Both want to be boss. We see the poorest commitment from players who allow their caddies to make the decisions or let them instill doubt about the golfers' own choices as they prepare to hit their shots. The greatest working relationships are those in which the player is receptive to a competent caddie's information, yet is ready to make his own decisions. For example, Dave Stockton—who is just above average on self-sufficiency—and his caddie, Todd Newcomb, have an arrangement that encourages Todd's involvement but allows Dave to make a full commitment to his own decisions. As they approach a shot, both Dave and Todd step off yardages and gather information. Todd gives Dave two suggested clubs and methods for executing the shot based on his information and his knowledge of Dave's game. Dave makes his choice considering his own information and that given to him by Todd. Todd fully supports and encourages Dave's decision even if he does not fully agree with it.

Because most players do not have the luxury of working with professional caddies who have had several years to get to know the players' game, many often find commitment comes easier when their caddies remain prepared to give advice but say nothing unless asked. But whatever method of involvement you choose, just make sure it allows you to be fully committed to your shots.

SELF-SUFFICIENCY AND TEACHING

Group-oriented players often are drawn to multiple teachers or can be too reliant on a single instructor. Interestingly, the greatest instructors have always encouraged and taught more self-reliance, so you should seek one who will help you learn to sort out your own problems, organize your own practice, and strategize your own game plans. Self-sufficiency comes easier to the player who is committed to his fundamentals for a long time—and to the instructor who teaches them.

That said, the journal mentioned earlier can help reduce your dependency on an instructor. You may be surprised at how good you can get at "tuning up" your own skills, allowing you to use your teacher for the more complex problems and the further development of your game. The resulting self-reliance will be very valuable to you when you need it the most.

If you think you are too self-sufficient, remember: Allow yourself to be coached. Even the best players in the world need and benefit from the assistance of others. To make this easier, carefully screen who's available and select someone who you respect and who best understands you and your style of play. It's much easier to listen to advice from someone who'll adapt his or her teaching style to your playing style, rather than the reverse.

Make a great effort to remain open-minded. Pretending you are a neutral observer when hearing the information often helps. Imagine the suggestions are being made to someone else before responding to them.

Resist withdrawing from others while stressed. The self-sufficient person at times feels such a strong need to resolve his own problems he will often withdraw from others. But this makes the self-sufficient more likely to bury issues than resolve them. This then triggers increased tension, increased emotions, and an inability to focus. Suggestion: Seek out at least one person with whom you can discuss problems and frustrations. This is imperative. Your confidant does not have to be a golfer. If you cannot find this in a friend, seek the assistance of a licensed therapist.

PERSONALIZATION:
Annette DeLuca

Annette DeLuca, a skilled athlete from North Bergen, New Jersey, did not start playing golf until the age of eighteen. But she learned the game quickly and turned professional within three years.

Much of her competitive experience was actually garnered during her several years on the minitours, which was very trying for her since she tested only moderately self-sufficient. It was particularly difficult when she played the Asian Tour in 1993. Nonetheless, her mental and physical athletic strengths pulled her through. She played the Gold Coast Tour in 1994 and 1995—winning two titles in the second year—and qualified for the U.S. Women's Open both of those years.

We met Annette near the end of her second year on the LPGA Tour, after she was referred to me by Jill Briles-Hinton, a friend and fellow competitor who felt that Annette had not played to her potential either year. She had played ten events the first year and twenty the second year, but had finished 189th and 167th, respectively, on the money list.

Annette took our personality test. We developed her profile and then discussed her recent play. We knew she was a great athlete, and her scores showed clearly that she was a fast learner. She tested to have high abstract abilities, good self-discipline, above-average dominance/competitiveness, and a moderate level of self-sufficiency that allowed her to openly accept the guidance of very qualified instructors, including Dr. Gary Wiren and Mike Adams. She showed few weaknesses on the Gold Coast Tour, but that was not the case on the LPGA Tour. Here she showed weakness in several areas, one of which was self-sufficiency. Annette came to recognize that she responded to play on the LPGA Tour by doing what comes a bit more naturally to her personality—allowing her caddies to be heavily involved in her decision-making. They were, after all, much more experienced on the Tour. They knew the courses, having walked them with other players many times. In hindsight, what she recognized was that in many situations she was hitting the ball without a full commitment.

For example, there were times when she wanted to hit a three-wood from the tee but, because she was a long hitter, her caddie would insist on her hitting a driver to "get around that corner." She would accept his decision, but then would "put a lazy swing on it," as she described it, and mishit the shot.

Annette committed to several mental goals for 1998, including increasing her self-sufficiency—principally by ensuring that final decisions were hers and that she would fully commit to every decision she made. She went on to finish her 1998 season earning $59,698, more than five times her previous year's earnings. She posted a new career-best finish with a tie for 11th at the McDonald's Championship and recorded a new career-best scoring average of 73.42. She wasn't yet taking the Tour by storm, but by becoming more self-sufficient, she was making tremendous progress.

Eight

Optimum Arousal

○

△

"A veritable demon seems to enter a golfer on the links . . . what otherwise would cause a golfer to transgress from even the most elementary rules . . . such as keeping the eye on the ball . . . or refraining from 'pressing' or hurrying the stroke?"

Arnold Haultain and Herbert Warren Wind, *The Mystery of Golf*

Everyone has experienced it. The game you've worked so hard to develop suddenly deserts you. Something alien has taken control of your body. Your mind starts to race, your breathing gets quick, your hands begin to strangle your club. Touch, feel, tempo, timing, decision-making skills—they're all there one moment but gone the next. Arnold Haultain and Herbert Wind liken the phenomenon to a demon entering the golfer's body. But what really is being experienced is a heightened state of arousal.

"Arousal," as we refer to it here, describes several things, including your muscular tension; physiological states related to heart rate, blood pressure, skin temperature, brain waves and breathing; and psychological states related to anxiety, worry, dread, excitement, and fear.

Golf, like every sport, requires that you maintain what is referred to by most sports psychologists as an "optimum level of arousal" for peak performance. It is one of the most important of the eight champion traits because, without it, all of the other physical and mental skills, no matter how strong they may be, are diminished. As Bobby Jones once said, "Golf is not exacting upon the physical powers of a man but it is trying upon his nerves, and the nervous strain usually reacts in some way upon the physical body."

The key to managing your arousal is your ability to manage stress-related tension. While muscular tension is obviously necessary to accomplish all movement and action, the actual levels of muscular tension and the physiological and psychological responses to stress can be managed in order to perform the task at hand.

In describing rounds, our tour clients often refer to "good tension" and "bad tension." Without the butterflies and excitement of the good tension that gives them the needed focus, tempo, and desire to compete, players find themselves playing underaroused, with a lax swing, little drive, and poor focus. Playing with bad tension, on the other hand, leaves players feeling stiff, rushed, and bound by a tight body and an overwrought mind.

The big difference? *Good tension is an arousal level that you can channel and control. Bad tension is an arousal level that is controlling you.*

To understand optimum arousal and why managing tension is so important, you must first understand how stress-related tension affects your physiological and psychological states of arousal.

Our bodies are designed to alter functions so that we have the best chance of survival when faced with life-threatening situations. Dr. Walter B. Cannon, who was a professor of physiology at the Harvard Medical School in the early part of this century, first described these changes as a "fight-or-flight response"—nature's way of preparing animals (including humans) to either run or fight. Most of us would find that we would run faster and harder than we knew we were capable of were we to come face-to-face with a dangerous animal or some other life-threatening situation. Physiological changes are triggered by hormones our bodies release in the face of danger.

The key here, however, is that the body does not know the difference between *real* and *perceived* danger. For example, your life is not truly in danger when you hit your first tee shot of a major tournament in front of a crowd, yet your body responds the same as it might if you suddenly realized you were standing on that tee surrounded by poisonous snakes.

Several things happen when you encounter real or perceived danger:

You release hormones: Initially epinephrine (adrenaline) and norepinephrine are released to jump-start your system by producing more blood sugar and raising your heart rate. Later, endorphins are released to numb pain and injury. In the early stages you feel energized, perhaps even having to club down a bit to adjust for the extra length you suddenly possess. But unless you manage your arousal, your clubs will come to feel like unwieldy sticks in your hand and your brain and/or body will feel exhausted, sometimes before the completion of your round.

It's not unusual for great players to be in continuously aroused states. It's because of the pressure to perform. Experiencing prolonged stress from golf or other issues, such as relationship, financial, or business strife, can exhaust the adrenal glands, create chronic fatigue, depress moods, and greatly reduce performance to a point of inducing slumps.

Your heart races: As pulse and blood pressure climb, more fuel is carried to your important muscles and major organs, especially your brain. Prolonged arousal can make your hands and feet feel cold, stiff, or numb since the blood that normally would have flowed there has been rerouted. This, along with muscle tension or alignment, leads players to feel uncomfortable with their setup, usually without really knowing why.

Your metabolism speeds up: There is a more efficient conversion of fuel to energy, increasing available blood sugar, which makes you feel supercharged while it lasts and very tired when it's gone.

You need to go to the toilet: As your metabolism speeds up, you want to relieve yourself more often. In fact, some players judge how nervous they are before a round by how many times they have to visit the toilet. What's happening is that your body is trying to lighten its load so it can run faster and jump higher to get away from those "snakes" on the first tee.

You feel nauseous: Some players find it difficult to eat before and during the round. Again the body is trying to free itself of excess weight and divert energy normally used for digestion to functions for survival.

Your mouth dries up: As energy for digestion is diverted, the production of saliva is slowed. Players who remain overaroused in competition will have unusually high levels of prolonged energy, but it manifests itself in a dry mouth and later, because of the lack of proper digestion, constipation.

Your muscles tense up: They receive a signal from the brain that danger is at hand and receive a surge of oxygen-rich blood. At the instant your muscles are alerted, your impulse is either to run away as fast as possible or to fight. But golf allows neither. So this muscle tension must instead be managed, and all energies must be channeled into concentration and focus. The tension also must be released because holding on to it inhibits the swing. Releasing it by aggression, however—destroying tee markers, kicking bags, breaking clubs—can actually leave the player with a shaky "adrenaline hangover," a sore toe, and if that player is a touring professional, a hefty fine.

Your breathing quickens and gets shorter: As muscle tension builds, chest muscles can constrict, causing you to take shorter quicker breaths. Overaroused players will often unknowingly hold their breath as they execute a shot or putt, usually resulting in an awkward steering and a mis-hit.

TENSION

"It's so frustrating because I'm hitting the ball great but can't play because of the extreme pain in my shoulder and the bulging disk in my neck. I recognize that they are stress-related. During my rehab I'm also going to get better at relaxing and simplifying my life."

Maggie Will

The best golfers always monitor their bodies for tension and take steps to manage arousal, and it's no coincidence that the champions usually are the best at maintaining optimum arousal levels during competition.

Since most players are not naturally aware of their arousal, we teach them to watch for physical signs of tension. We see these signals all the time when we watch them play.

Their heads tilt forward, putting strain on their necks. Their shoulders tighten. Their arms are held closer to the body, and their hands tighten into fists, fidget with coins or other objects, or grip the clubs too tightly.

Their torsos become rigid and lean more forward, often straining the lower back. Their teeth clinch and their lips tighten. Those chewing gum start to chew rapidly. The muscles around their eyes are more strained and their brows become furrowed. And, as noted before, their breaths become quicker and shorter.

These physical changes usually result in swings that are quicker and shorter and putting strokes that more resemble a punch, pull, or push. As we have mentioned, average players all too often misdiagnose their swing problems as mechanical when the real problem is overarousal. The mechanics are breaking down under pressure, but they often return when the player gets more relaxed.

THE CHAMPION GOLFER

"The most unpropitious symptom I can experience before an important round of match or medal play is absence of nervousness."

Bobby Jones

As part of our effort to determine optimum arousal levels, we measured the tension levels of professionals of varying abilities. On a scale of one-to-ten, 1 being relaxed and 10 being tense, the champion golfers measure in the middle. More important, they are able to maintain the same or slightly higher levels of tension when they compete.

To put this in perspective, we compared optimum arousal levels for golf to optimum arousal levels for other sports, using the same one-to-ten scale. We found that, if golf measures 4 to 6, other sports rate as follows:

Baseball—3 to 7
Basketball—4 to 8
Football—6 to 9
Power lifting—8 to 9
Hockey—6 to 9
Target shooting—2 to 3

Most sports require a range of levels. The defensive lineman needs a greater surge of adrenaline as he executes a play than, for example, the quarterback. In basketball, shooting a free throw requires a lower level of arousal than what is needed for successfully executing a fast break. The same goes in golf. As a general rule, tasks that require more gross motor skills—such as your long game—require higher arousal and those that require more fine motor skills—like your short game—require lower arousal. For the long game, you will want to manage your arousal to around a 6. Your arousal should be at its lowest, at around a 4, when executing your short game, to maintain your feel and the use of fine motor skills.

In fact, when someone comes to us with a putting problem—especially the many golfers who have come to us with the yips—one of the first things we check is that player's arousal on and around the greens. Invariably we find that, instead of getting more relaxed as he approaches the greens, he is unknowingly getting more aroused. This is typically the result of many things, including his perception of himself as a putter, the pressure he is putting on himself to score, an over-awareness of score and outcome, and such emotions as excitement, fear, or dread.

It's much less common for golfers to compete while in an underaroused state. But it does happen. Players become too relaxed. Their minds wander. Mental preparation is poor. They swing without real purpose and are lax in course management.

Some golfers are more relaxed because of temperament, but more often it's because of boredom; they have little motivation or purpose. We find this is fairly common with touring professionals who have been competing for more than a decade and with amateurs who have played for years with the same people on the same courses, all of whom are playing without having set clear, measurable, and motivating goals. Fatigue and illness play roles, too, as does that feeling of exasperation that can induce some players to quit trying during a frustrating round.

Signs of low arousal include:

○ A wandering mind: Players lazily gather only partial information for each shot or putt and are distracted by rambling thoughts or outside variables, such as the time of day, what they plan to have for dinner, or a conversation they may just have had.
○ Poor focus: Concentration and commitment are weak. Players can't keep their heads in the game.

○ Boredom: Players have little stimulation or motivation to play well.

○ A lack of involvement: Feeling more like a spectator than a participant, players just go through the motions rather than immersing themselves in the matter at hand.

Many, many golfers play when overaroused. Woody Austin, the 1995 PGA Rookie of the Year, once said, "My physical game is as good as it can be . . . I can hit about any shot I need to hit. . . . What I need to be able to do better is turn off my brain and calm myself when I'm in position." This is a common refrain for a lot of golfers. They rush to the first tee with nary a break in stride, whisk through a quick warm-up, and start playing without ever settling themselves. It's not unusual for them to play the entire round overaroused, sometimes never recognizing the tension that is sabotaging their play.

Professionals do the same but for different reasons. The competition itself usually raises their arousal, especially when they are playing in major championships, playing in contention, or playing very poorly. If they do not take steps to manage their arousal before they tee off, no matter how much time they may have, there is little chance they will manage their arousal while they play. They end up gripping their clubs tighter and swinging faster. Their minds race. They have too little touch and feel and little or no patience.

Greg Norman went through this during his final round at the 1996 Masters. He did a remarkable job of managing his arousal for three full days, opening up a six-stroke lead over the field. But he couldn't keep it up through the fourth day. He shot a 78 to turn a seemingly insurmountable lead into a five-stroke loss.

Greg needed enormous mental discipline to manage his arousal that day, a tall order given that Greg has a naturally high level of arousal, drive, and intensity. Ironically, his drive and intensity are what make him so successful and so popular. And most of the time, he's very good at managing his arousal so that it doesn't affect his game. So what happened that Sunday at the Masters?

Greg was leading one of the most prestigious events in the world, one in which he had finished runner-up or at least in contention more than any other golfer in recent memory, so it was a title he dearly wanted to win. And he had been handling a continuous barrage of outcome questions—which led to outcome thoughts—that were only intensified by his huge lead. Toss in the fact that he was playing one of the more challenging courses in the world—it punishes even the slightest error—and that the whole golf world was watching to see if Greg Norman could finally get the monkey off his back.

So you begin to understand the situation. Overarousal was evident on the first tee, but instead of easing as the round progressed, the tension seemed to climb, preventing him from maintaining a peaceful focus or a commitment to his game plan.

Butch Harmon, his instructor at the time, said later that Greg seemed to "lose the rhythm" of his swing, "got faster" on his putts, and "walked faster." Tellingly, he also noted that, "Mechanically, I did not see a lot wrong."

Mechanics weren't Greg Norman's primary problem on that fateful Sunday. His level of arousal was.

DO YOU GET TOO AROUSED?

This is an area where an acquaintance may know us better than we know ourselves. You may therefore want to consult with a friend, golf instructor, or family member in determining where you may rate with this trait.

What Are Your Tendencies?

Compare your tendencies to those listed in this simple chart. Keep in mind that 1 represents someone who is extremely relaxed; 10 represents someone who is extremely tense; and 5 to

6 represents someone who is a combination of the two traits, or who is "average" in both. Estimate at which point of this scale you might score on this trait based on *your* personal and golfing tendencies, then circle that number.

When asked to rate personal states of arousal or tension, most of us are not as insightful as a well-acquainted observer. For this reason, you might want to consult with a friend, teacher, or family member to estimate where you may fall on this scale.

Relaxed									Tense
1	2	3	4	5	6	7	8	9	10

PERSONAL TENDENCIES:

Carefree	Worried
Calm	Stressed
Low drive	High drive
Mind wanders	Mind races
Peaceful	Intense
Couch potato	Workaholic
Unhurried	Rushed
Lethargic	Fidgety
Easily "kicks back"	Has difficulty relaxing

GOLFING TENDENCIES:

Underaroused for competition	Overaroused for competition
Consistent, smooth tempo	Irregular, fast tempo
Visualization underused	Visualization skills overwhelmed
Patient acceptance of mistakes	Impatient with mistakes
Methodical	Rushed
Mind wanders	Mind races
Tendency to underpractice	Tendency to overpractice

The champions are, or strive to be, a nice balance between relaxed and tense.

Players Who Have a Tendency Toward Under-Arousal

As we mentioned, players who naturally test low in arousal tend to be rare, but they do exist, even among touring professionals. Depending somewhat on their other traits (since confidence, emotional stability, and other traits do influence reactions to stress), they can have laid-back styles, slower tempos, or better short games. Fred Couples, Loren Roberts, Emlyn Aubrey, and Julie Piers have slightly lower arousal levels than most golfers. Such players must keep clear, measurable, and motivating goals to be competitive. They also are prone to misinterpretation when their lower states of arousal are confused with low desire or lack of competitiveness. Nothing could be further from the truth.

Loren Roberts, nicknamed "Boss of the Moss" by fellow pro David Ogrin because of his putting prowess, has a relaxed (although very competitive) personality and is a good example of a player who knows himself well. He turned professional in 1981 and for thirteen years motivated himself with many performance goals to support his ultimate outcome goal of achieving his first Tour victory. When it finally came in 1994, Loren had the wisdom to step back and establish a new goal for himself even before playing in his next event. He needed something that would give him the drive, the focus and the sense of purpose he needed to stay in top shape mentally during the remaining two-thirds of his year. He set several challenging but reachable goals, including a top-10 ranking. Loren went on to complete the year with a total of nine top-ten and twelve top-twenty-five finishes, allowing him to reach a position of sixth on the 1994 money list.

Players Who Have a Tendency Toward Overarousal

Most of our clients test to be overaroused for golf, or they at least become so in competitive situations. You may or may not have noticed it, but many great players continually work to tame their arousal in an effort to play their best golf. Such players include Greg Norman, Mark McCumber, Brandie Burton, Mark Calcavecchia, Woody Austin, Phil Blackmar, Nanci Bowen, and Michelle McGann. And even players who always look as though they are perfectly calm—Mike Reid and Tom Purtzer, to name two—must monitor mind and body to maintain an optimum level of arousal. All these players, and many others like them, are known for their intensity and drive to succeed.

The techniques recommended in this chapter have been used by them and other Tour players in various combinations to manage arousal on and off the course. We suggest you consider them all, then choose those that are most effective and comfortable for you.

HOW AROUSED ARE YOU?

While this questionnaire is intended to increase your awareness and achievement of optimum arousal levels for golf, we hope you will find it helps in other areas of your life as well.

Begin with this quick rating of your tension, or arousal, in the most competitive situations in which you find yourself. In previous ratings, we've considered only one set of questions, but in this case it is important to consider both your high and low levels of arousal, because we find that some players actually fluctuate between the two. Apply the point values based on the following scale:

1: Always   2: Often   3: Sometimes   4: Seldom   5: Never

Low Arousal

___ A. My mind wanders as I prepare to hit shots or putts.
___ B. I find myself losing interest in my round—perhaps even feeling somewhat bored.

___ C. I have found myself not caring how I play, maybe because if I do care I will be disappointed.

___ D. I am told I do not work hard enough at my game.

___ E. I play without goals.

_____ Total x 2 ÷ 5 = _____ Low Arousal Rating

If you rated yourself 8 or higher, underarousal should not be a problem. If you rated lower than 8, you should learn how to manage or elevate your arousal.

High Arousal

___ A. I am told I have a tendency to get quick with my swing.

___ B. I am told I decelerate when putting or jab at my putts.

___ C. I try but have difficulty visualizing my shots or putts.

___ D. I find I am very impatient with myself and/or others.

___ E. I have recurring pain in my back, shoulders, neck, or head.

___ F. After finishing my rounds, I feel mentally exhausted.

___ G. I have been known to overpractice or try too hard.

_____ Total x 2 ÷ 7 = _____ High Arousal Rating

If you rated yourself 8 or higher, your arousal level shouldn't be a problem. If you rated lower than 8, you should learn how to lower your level of arousal.

Players who have arousal fluctuations during rounds often follow a pattern. They start the round overaroused, anxious, and nervous and, without realizing it, try too hard to perform. Poor performance discourages and frustrates, leaving them feeling their efforts are pointless. Then they relax or "give in" to a level that feels they are not trying—and suddenly their performance improves.

Unfortunately, this better play renews their excitement. Soon they are back into an overaroused state, trying too hard, and cycling back into their discouraged and frustrated mode. And so it goes.

Other golfers play in an overaroused state for so long that it can feel natural to them. They may unintentionally reach an ideal level of arousal not because of conscious efforts to relax but as a result of illness, fatigue, injury, or competing in extremely hot and humid conditions. A line frequently quoted by many Tour players goes something like this: "Beware of the sick or injured golfer." Sickness or injury prevents them from getting overaroused, while their natural competitiveness keeps their arousal level up. Where the two arousal levels meet is close to the optimum level.

MANAGING YOUR AROUSAL LEVEL

In this section we will teach you how to manage your arousal for peak performance considering problems with both under and overarousal. The vast majority of players need techniques to lower their arousal, so most of this section will be devoted to that. But there is always a need for techniques that will help raise arousal, particularly on those days when you may feel unmotivated or have trouble concentrating. We'll deal with managing underarousal first.

Managing Underarousal

Most of us have rounds during which our minds wander, we feel sluggish, or we just have a hard time getting motivated to play even close to our best. What follows are techniques to use either on the course during competition, during casual rounds, or during practice that will help you raise your level of arousal.

Exercise

In addition to the stretching exercises that you should do, take about ten minutes before each round to elevate your heart rate. Just as exercise can calm the overaroused, so it can stimulate the underaroused. Some players jog, cycle, or stair-climb, while others simply run in place for a few minutes to increase blood flow and stimulate the release of endorphins.

Goal-setting

Outcome goals—winning the club championship, for example—should be considered long-term, but how you achieve them should be via a series of daily performance goals. These should represent what can be accomplished that day, using imagery to clearly see your target before as many shots as possible, perhaps, or being conscious of keeping your optimum level of arousal for the entire round.

Gambling

While we cannot recommend gambling for high stakes, having something riding on the round can help raise arousal to effective levels. It may help you to focus and care about doing your mental routine effectively. This is not as good as setting controllable and achievable goals, but it may help you get through a round you would otherwise be unmotivated to play.

Managing Overarousal

How you respond to real and perceived stress has a tremendous impact on your golf game and your life. We encourage you to explore different methods until you find those that suit you best.

Body Checks

Take a few moments several times a day to scan your body for tension. Remain particularly aware of locations where you're most likely to feel tension, such as the shoulders, neck, abdomen, jaw, face, back. You also can scan for some of the physical signs mentioned earlier in the chapter, such as drawn shoulders, clenched fists, tight face, or furrowed brow.

On the golf course, the best times to scan your body are on the first tee, as you approach particularly difficult shots, around the greens, or anytime you are in a situation that is challenging to you.

Deep Breathing

Once you have identified areas of tension, stretch and relax these areas. Next, take some deep "diaphragmatic" breaths. A diaphragmatic breath is drawn from the abdominal areas, as opposed to a "thoracic" breath, which is drawn from the chest. Thoracic breathing is most common when we are overaroused. As our body tightens our breathing gets shallower and more rapid, and our heart rate increases to overcome the reduction in oxygen. This triggers our stress response. Diaphragmatic breathing, on the other hand, comes naturally to us in our relaxed states—it's how we breathe when we sleep. Air is pulled deep into the lungs as the diaphragm expands and is exhaled as it contracts. This is said to trigger our relaxation response.

The best way to practice diaphragmatic breathing is to place a hand on your abdomen, and inhale deeply, pushing your hand out, then exhale slowly by pressing your hand down on your abdomen. Repeat until your breathing is smooth, deep, and rhythmical.

Many golfers, including Jack Nicklaus, breathe deeply before or during their preshot routines, especially on days when tension is a persistent challenge. Those with putting problems should consciously take a full, deep breath the moment their feet make contact with the putting surface.

Becoming more aware of your breathing and learning to use more diaphragmatic breaths are among the easiest and most effective techniques you can use to reduce your arousal both on and off the course.

Nutrition

The links between food and anxiety have been well documented for more than a decade. Some foods and supplements can help produce a calmer state, while others can create additional stress and arousal. Some of us are more influenced by what we eat than others, but all of us can better manage our arousal if we know what helps and hurts our efforts.

Caffeine stimulates you by increasing the neurotransmitters in your brain, sympathetic nervous system activity, and the release of adrenaline—the same reactions that occur when your body responds to stress! Caffeine is found in coffee, tea, and many soft drinks, as well as in such over-the-counter drugs as Vivarin, Excedrin, Anacin, and No-Doz. All elevate your arousal.

Nicotine, contrary to what many smokers think, is a stimulant. It makes the heart work harder and in some cases increases shortness of breath.

Such amphetamine-like drugs as Ritalin, Benzedrine, or Dexedrine increase anxiety levels by activating the brain and elevating alertness and concentration.

Too much salt from processed and snack foods, as well as salt we add to our foods, stresses the body by depleting potassium, a mineral necessary for the nervous system, and by increasing blood pressure.

Moderate to large amounts of simple sugars in beverages, cereals, cookies, candies, processed juices, and the like can lead to extreme fluctuations in blood sugar, which can trigger anxiety, palpitations, irritability, and trembling.

Excessive alcohol can elevate blood pressure, deplete vitamin B, and cause fluctuations in blood sugar, all making management of arousal difficult, particularly with long term use.

In addition, skipping meals, eating large meals, and eating too fast all compromise your abilities to digest your food and maintain steady productions of blood sugar for energy. As blood sugar fluctuates, tendencies toward anxiety can increase or become difficult to manage.

We strongly encourage you to start to improve your eating habits by keeping a food diary for several days to a week. Document everything, including all snacks, drinks, pills, and supplements. It helps to also make note of your moods and feelings of calmness. Most people are surprised when they take a closer look at their nutritional habits. They are usually taken aback at how bad they are, but at least they can easily identify where there's room for improvement.

Supplements

Prolonged stress or arousal tends to rapidly deplete the amount of vitamins in the body—and especially those vitamins most important for resisting stress. People with highly competitive careers or stressful lifestyles, including professional golfers, are vulnerable to experiencing low resistance to stress because of vitamin deficiencies, even if their diets are otherwise satisfactory. Supplements can help compensate. Those we often recommend include vitamin C, vitamin B complex, multiple vitamins, calcium, magnesium, relaxation herbs, and various amino acids. All help stimulate or control your levels of arousal. You can contact us directly or visit our website for more detailed recommendations.

Note: While we do not encourage the use of medication to manage arousal, we are often asked about it in seminars, workshops, and individual sessions. The players we have seen who better manage their arousal with the help of medication are those who also experience major symptoms of depression or suffer from anxiety disorders. They manage their symptoms with one of many modern antidepressant medications but also incorporate some of the mental and physical changes recommended here.

Some players have come to us after experimenting with beta-adrenergic–blocking drugs, better known as "beta-blockers." These medications are nonaddictive and work by blocking certain actions of the sympathetic nervous system, effectively reducing physical symptoms of performance anxiety, such as heart palpitations, severe sweating, high blood pressure, and such. Beta-blockers do not change the psychological aspects of overarousal, and they do come with the possibility of considerable side effects, such as impotence, dizziness, fatigue, or drowsiness. Players who have used them have complained of not feeling like themselves and of losing important touch and feel. We believe that the only golfers who truly benefit from the use of beta-blockers are those who need them for other medical reasons.

Relaxation Techniques

Players who experience chronic tension in their bodies find that incorporating some method of relaxation each day really helps them manage their arousal and their health. There are several ways to go about this:

○ Progressive relaxation: This should take about ten minutes each day. Start by finding a quiet place with soft light where you can sit or lie down comfortably without being disturbed. Take a few deep diaphragmatic breaths to begin relaxing, then take your attention to your toes. Tighten the muscles in your toes as tightly as possible and hold for several seconds. Slowly and fully relax your toes. This is to start a wave of relaxation that you should imagine spreading slowly and progressively through your body. Now take your attention to the rest of your feet and repeat the tensing and relaxing, allowing the relaxed, warm feeling to spread to the next area of your body. Progress slowly and sequentially, focusing on tensing and relaxing the rest of your body—your ankles, calves, knees, thighs, hips, stomach, chest, arms, shoulders, neck, face, and eyes. When you have done this, scan your body for any remaining tension. If you find any, imagine that tension slowly melting, leaving your entire body warm, comfortable, and relaxed.

This relaxed state is a good time to practice imagery. Imagine yourself successfully playing a very difficult hole, for example. When the "session" is over, slowly open your eyes, stretch, and resume your day.

○ Relaxation tapes: GolfPsych has created a series of au-diotapes geared to encourage relaxation. While you will find many good relaxation tapes in most major book-stores, GolfPsych tapes have been created specifically for golfers. They are designed to guide you through sim-ple relaxation techniques as well as to teach you nu-merous GolfPsych lessons that will help you with your mental preparation.

○ Yoga: With its meditation, breathing, physical pos-tures, and exercises, yoga has long been used not only to increase flexibility and muscle tone but also as a stress reducer. Studies have found that doing yoga ex-ercises each day can lower blood pressure and heart rate, reduce pain, and improve memory, motor skills, metabolic rates, and respiratory function. If yoga classes are available in your area, you may want to sign up to improve your golf.

○ Qigong: Pronounced "chi-kung," this is an ancient Chinese exercise combining rhythmic breathing with smooth and graceful movements. Studies have shown that daily qigong exercises can lower your heart rate and blood pressure, reduce stress, and increase energy. In addition, many forms of martial arts—kung fu, judo, tae kwon do, aikido, kenseido, t'ai chi, hap ki do, and jujitsu—incorporate mind, body, and spiritual de-velopment that include great lessons for managing arousal. Check your phone book for martial arts cen-ters and classes in your area.

○ Therapeutic massage and stretching exercises: Massage can have a sedative effect on the nervous system as well as promote muscle relaxation. Various types of stretching exercises, particularly those recommended for golfers, are also helpful.

○ Exercise: Regular vigorous exercise is a great outlet for excess arousal in that it helps reduce your body's buildup of muscular tension and adrenaline. With your doctor's approval, choose one or more aerobic activities, sports, or exercises that you feel you can enjoy and incorporate into your lifestyle for an extended period of time.

○ Biofeedback: This is a way to learn how to regulate unconscious bodily functions, such as pulse, breathing, and blood pressure. It requires only a watch with a second hand. First, take your pulse by placing your index finger on your carotid artery, in the neck just below your ear, and counting the number of beats for ten seconds. Then multiply that number by six to find out your pulse. Record your pulse just before falling asleep or immediately upon waking, during an intense practice session, and just before playing a competitive round. This should give you a read of both your resting pulse, how much your pulse elevates for golf, and how much more it elevates for competition. You can round out your awareness—and probably surprise yourself—by checking your pulse after one of your more frustrating experiences.

Since it is important to maintain a relaxed heart rate during a round of golf, here's an example of a technique we use to achieve that goal: First practice lowering your heart rate during a practice session by taking a moment to take a deep breath, relax your body, and imagine yourself lying in bed, just about to fall asleep. Having done that, record your pulse again. Repeat until you have successfully lowered the rate.

Now imagine going to the first tee at Augusta National to play the first shot of the final round of the Masters. If your imagery is good, your pulse will be higher. Now relax by using your imagery of falling asleep and check your pulse again. With practice you will be able to use this or other relaxing imagery of your choice to lower your heart rate and arousal before and during a competitive round.

Thought Checks

As you may remember from Chapter 6, thought checks involve taking a few conscious moments to assess the quality of your thoughts. As a general rule, when you are feeling unsettled or tense, you are likely wasting mental energy in nonproductive areas, especially worrying about things that are out of your control. You should check your thoughts to see if they are productive and positive.

For example, before going into a round, are you thinking productively of things over which you have control, such as focusing on ideal targets, types of shots you want and feel you can hit, and strategies for handling adversity? Or are your thoughts unproductive and stressful, such as worrying about something you cannot change or that has not yet happened? Are you worrying about how difficult the course is playing, how hard the wind might blow, how low you need to shoot, or how well your opponents might play?

Before you start your round, make a list of items over which you have control that truly deserve your mental energies that day, such as committing to targets, visualizing all shots, feeling great tempo, deep breathing, taking mental breaks between shots, or using positive self-talk. Anytime you find yourself feeling overaroused or unsettled during the round, check your thoughts and replace them with something from your list that offers you more control and productive use of your mental energies.

Meditation or Prayer

Meditation has been practiced for several thousand years. In the last three decades, there has been considerable scientific study that has documented meditation's value as a tool for stress reduction.

Meditation has been defined as any activity that keeps your attention calmly fixed in the present moment.

There are two simple forms of meditation that we recommend. "Focused meditation" involves concentrating on one thing for a sustained period, such as your breathing, a sound, or an object. "Awareness meditation" involves opening your awareness to your immediate or imagined surroundings so that you become fully and calmly enveloped in the images, sounds, smells, feelings, and sensations of the moment.

There always are opportunities to use meditation techniques on the golf course. For example, as you walk to your ball you can use focused meditation by counting your relaxed, deep breaths. Or you can use awareness meditation by becoming very mentally aware of the feeling of the earth beneath each step, the shades of green in the landscape, the shapes of clouds or trees, or the feel of the sun or wind on your skin.

Guided Imagery

Many golfers find that imagery is not only a great technique for relaxing, but also a valuable, fast, and effective method for practicing various aspects of their games. Start by assuming a relaxed position and taking a few deep, relaxing breaths. Now imagine guiding or taking yourself to one of your most peaceful and relaxed places. For many this is a favorite vacation spot, a fondly remembered childhood location, or their own easy chair, bed or hammock. In as much detail as possible, see and experience the comfort and peacefulness of your chosen surroundings. Feel the comfort and peace you have experienced there for a few moments before getting up to resume your day.

With practice, going to your special place should get easier and faster. Once it does, you will be able to use this relaxed state and further guide your imagery to prepare for golf. For example, imagine taking yourself into your next round with this same peaceful, relaxed feeling. See yourself warming up your mental routine and your swing with this same relaxed state. Endeavor to mentally play the first hole with a peaceful focus that allows you to be very committed, with great pictures and feel of your shots. Imagine using your best natural tempo for each shot. When you are able, repeat the imagery for any other shot or hole that you find particularly challenging.

With enough practice, you will be able to go to your favorite place in the midst of one of your more aroused moments on the golf course and with your eyes wide open.

Mental Rehearsal

There are numerous players, including Jack Nicklaus, who use guided imagery to mentally rehearse playing their entire round of golf before going to the first tee. They imagine their chosen targets and clubs and see the shots they want to hit on each hole. If, during their mental rehearsal, their arousal rises, and it frequently does, they also mentally rehearse relaxing in that situation using deep breathing or their chosen method of calming themselves.

We've found that mental rehearsal helps a great deal when you're about to play a course you have had little opportunity to practice on or on which you are very uncomfortable and indecisive. It also helps when you are about to play in situations that likely will increase your arousal, such as an intimidating playing partner or while in contention or in the lead of a tournament.

Once on the course, you can use mental rehearsal if you are uncomfortable with a shot but have hit that type of shot well in practice or competition. Just rehearse hitting that shot as you did in your previous circumstances before stepping up to the ball.

Music

Many find it easiest to relax to music. Set aside ten minutes or more, especially on your busiest days, to put yourself in a comfortable position with eyes closed to quietly listen to some of your favorite, calming music. Stay as mentally involved with the music as possible. Classical music, especially baroque, is usually recommended, but any relatively soft music seems as effective so long as you find it pleasant and soothing. Music that is arousing and stimulating with lively instrumentation and lyrics is usually best saved for those days when your arousal is low.

Some players even use music when on the golf course. Fuzzy Zoeller, Brad Fabel, and Mark McCumber all hum or whistle between shots. Dick Zokol, a Tour pro, has worn headphones and listened to tapes of music on the course. During your most aroused moments, consciously relax your body and try softly humming or whistling your tune. Players with great imagery skills, who choose not to be so obvious, simply imagine hearing one of their favorite songs in their mind's ear.

Time Management and Personal Balance

Keeping your life well balanced and organized is a great help in managing arousal. To teach balance, we encourage players to plan quantity and quality time for five specific areas of their lives: career, personal, family, relationship, and friends.

Part of staying organized is learning to budget your time so that you effectively manage and maximize your abilities in each of these areas. This involves many skills, such as resolving conflicts, maintaining quality relationships, organizing practice and play, and ensuring health and personal growth.

The Importance of Mental Rest

Mental fatigue tends to skew your arousal. Physical fatigue can do the same, but you generally know when to rest your body. Two key signs of mental fatigue are impatience and a reduced ability to focus. That's why we often recommend that our pro golfer clients play no more than three to five weeks in a row, depending largely on how they balance their time.

Mental fatigue also plays a role late in a round. If you have been working too hard mentally from the beginning of the round, you will not have enough mental energy to finish the round. Your level of arousal will have been too high for too long and you will make poor decisions and perform poorly. Don't be surprised. Most humans just cannot stay focused for four hours and more.

The solution is to take mental breaks between shots. Think about things that you find relaxing and interesting. Focus on your breathing. Do anything you can think of that will lower your arousal until it is time to play your next shot. Then, as you begin the calculation stage of your routine, your focus will narrow and arousal will rise enough to play the shot. How long you should rest mentally will become clear the more you do it. This differs from golfer to golfer.

PERSONALIZATION:
Lee Janzen

Lee came into the 1998 U.S. Open at Olympic feeling good about his game and wanting to win this tournament more than any other. His physical game was working well, and although he'd had a few problems finishing some tournaments earlier in the year—in the Players Championship and the Houston Open—his mental game was in pretty good shape, too.

It had been almost three years since his last tour victory, and he had probably gotten a little too excited or aroused during the last round of the Players Championship, where he lost a five-stroke lead. The same had happened at the Houston Open, where Lee missed four putts of six feet or less while in the lead.

Memories like those two recent tourneys can cause any player to question their nerve and ability to stay in control when they are in a similar situation. Those memories can shake both performance confidence and personal confidence—if you allow them to.

Lee refused to allow those failures to shake his personal confidence. He chose to look at them philosophically, affirming that he could play better and in the future he would. They would not be allowed to hurt his chances or his future. He also took a hard look at his putting and determined that his alignment was slightly off.

Lee started the final round of the 1998 U.S. Open five strokes back of Payne Stewart and in the third-to-last group. His mental approach at the time demonstrates his golf maturity. "I wasn't thinking about winning when I teed off," he says. "I figured I'd be too nervous if I thought about that. I went out and tried to play a good round of golf."

Early in the round, after bogeying the second and third hole, Lee fell seven strokes behind Payne. "When I bogeyed two and three," he said, "my first thought was to just hit good shots, and then, if I have some good holes maybe I can get back into this thing. I didn't count myself out, but I wasn't thinking about winning."

On the fifth hole Lee got a break. After hitting his ball into a tree, he declared it lost and decided to hit another. Having just birdied the fourth hole, Lee thought that this was an awfully bad break, but before he hit the second ball and before the five minutes he was allowed to look for the first one had expired, it fell out of the tree! At this moment, Lee really began to feel confident and relaxed.

Lee had been able to get away with watching the scoreboards all week without falling victim to outcome-thinking. But upon looking at the scoreboard on the twelfth hole, Lee felt a surge of adrenaline as he realized he was within striking distance of winning the tournament. He knew also that his reaction to the moment was crucial: He could let his excitement and awareness soar, interfering with focus and arousal, or he could take special steps to manage it by no longer checking out the scoreboards.

"Playing the golf part is easy," he said afterward, "because we've done it so many times. But keeping your emotions in check is the hard part. And after eleven, I realized I had a chance to win. And I kept thinking: This is the U.S. Open. I have a chance to win. I had to keep reminding myself that it only takes one shot. If I lose focus, I could ruin my chance of winning. That's really what kept me going. I just said when this thing is over, you can relax and think about all the great things. But every shot—if you don't give your full attention to every shot, you're not going to win this thing.

"I'd looked at the scoreboard the entire week," Lee continued, "but I just made a point to myself on the thirteenth hole that I would not look at the scoreboard the rest of the day. I didn't want to know how I stood. I was going to play my game the rest of the way in. I didn't want to think if I got lucky and got ahead . . . and I didn't want to play safe. I just wanted to continue to hit good shots."

This is a wonderful example of a player understanding the pitfalls of thinking about the wrong things and choosing to focus on the process of playing golf. He knew that if he thought too much of winning the tournament his emotions and his arousal would peak and his play would deteriorate. Even though he made two bogeys early, he stayed mentally tough, making four birdies and finishing the round at 68, two under par.

Of the top twenty-four finishers in the 1998 U.S. Open, only Lee Janzen broke par on Sunday. The other players in contention had played very well the first three days, but on the final day, when it mattered most, they had difficulty managing their arousal and controlling their thoughts well enough to play the last round to the best of their abilities.

Lee Janzen had won his second U.S. Open Championship—proving once again the importance of a strong mental game.

Epilogue

As you complete your first (we hope) of several passes through *The 8 Traits of Champion Golfers,* we trust that you already have greater insight into the aspects of your personality that are your strengths and your weaknesses for the game.

Whether your aspirations are as simple as a greater enjoyment of the game or as lofty as becoming a world-class golfer, we feel certain that the techniques we have outlined in this book, combined with your own desire and motivation, can help you achieve your goals.

Supporting this belief is the frequent and unsolicited positive feedback on our web-site, where players and coaches can download our quarterly newsletter or order the questionnaire and report. This feedback comes from a wide variety of people in various parts of the world—most of whom we have never met—and with differing levels of involvement with the sport.

One enthusiastic e-mail came from fairly close to home and was sent by Robert W. Prentiss of St. Charles High School. He wrote to say that he has back issues of and subscribes to the

GolfPsych Newsletter. And he stated that he has "stressed 'thinking like a champion' for several years, but it is great to now have your newsletters as a reference. My guys won the [1998 Illinois State Championship] tournament by 17 shots (36 holes) in terrible weather conditions. A great testament to their mental toughness."

Another e-mail came from Tom Zoretic of Bowling Green, Kentucky, after he had ordered and taken the questionnaire, reviewed his GolfPsych Profile, and read his GolfPsych Report. "I have never felt more confident about my game—it even strengthened my physical game. Your report about me was the key that unlocked my ability and allowed me to pass the PAT [Player Ability Test for the PGA's Golf Professional Training Program] and start my career in the golf industry. I look forward to becoming a Class A PGA Professional, then attending your GolfPsych instructor school so I can share this with everyone I know."

Also supporting our belief in the methods that we teach is the continued progress of so many of our professional and amateur clients. You may remember Annette DeLuca from Chapter 7. She started working with us, and in 1998 we saw her increase her yearly earnings on the LPGA Tour by more than five times, making $59,698. Two months into the 1999 season, after a second place finish in the Hawaiian Ladies Open, she was ranked thirteenth on the money list with $56,966. Annette is well on her way to her goal of being a champion on the LPGA Tour.

Our greatest reward, beyond hearing of or seeing our clients achieve their goals, is the greater sense of peace and happiness that they attain in the process.

It is our hope that this book will be a catalyst to helping you do the same.